Shelter

BOBBIE GERBER

A Work of Ministry

THE SEABURY PRESS | NEW YORK

1983
The Seabury Press
815 Second Avenue
New York, N.Y. 10017

Library of Congress Cataloging in Publication Data

Gerber, Bobbie, 1942-
Shelter: a work of ministry.

1. Church work with youth—Michigan—Kalamazoo.
2. Gerber, Bobbie, 1942-   . I. Title.
BV4447.G47   1983   259'.23'0977418   83-8984
ISBN 0-8164-2622-8

To saints and fools —
wherever they may be

Acknowledgments

I would like to express my sincere thanks to all who helped in the preparation of this book: To Jerry Diment of the Eighth Day Bookstore who was helpful and encouraging in the beginning; to Jean Cox, Jane Collingsworth, Robert Hegel, Juli Formsma, Richard Jackson, and Carma Van Liere, who proofread various chapters for me; and to Barbara Cripe, Robert and Sally Hosack, Sharon and Nico Seinen, and Dan Stoepker for their contributions to the ministry and the information they provided.

My real teachers were the people who used the services of The Open Door and The Next Door and made the work exciting and interesting. I used fictitious names in the book for individuals I described and blurred some of the details by which they could be identified. Reconciliation and continued contact with those who gave me permission to tell their stories has been a source of great joy.

Contents

Preface

To write a book about my own ministry seemed at first a narcissistic endeavor. As I began, however, I realized that I was exposing my weaknesses as much as my strengths, my faults as much as my virtues, and not only a few good ideas but a lot of naive and unproductive ones. My hope is that readers will find humor in my mistakes, and perhaps learn from them. May it be a testimony that Christ's strength is made perfect in weakness, and his grace is sufficient for all.

Two main themes developed in the course of the writing. The first is that of motivation and inspiration to do the kind of work described. I always liked to quip that one had to be a saint or a fool to do it, and anyone who was merely a fool would not last long! Clearly, those of us who worked at Kalamazoo Youth Ministry were a little of both, saints in the sense that we offered up our lives by taking personal risks and sacrificing amenities, pride, and earning power; fools in the sense that we tackled situations we had no training or preparation to handle. Just as clearly there was a canopy of grace over us that protected us from harm and danger, and a net under us that kept us from falling into despair and enabled us to laugh when we felt most desperate. May those readers who are contemplating or presently engaged in a similar ministry feel less lonely and isolated as a result of this book. And may they be assured, in the words of Teilhard de Chardin, that ". . . little by little we shall see the universal horror relax, and smile at us, and enfold us in more-than-human arms."

The second theme is that of authority, the issue which can most quickly make or break a ministry of this kind. How long, for instance, could we take in anyone and everyone off the street, live with them day after day, and still maintain our health and sanity? How could those of us serving in the ministry work together as a team with widely divergent views on the meaning of the ministry and even more diverse personal needs? The danger in the first instance is constant resistance and rebellion on the part of those served; the danger in the second is the loss of competent and dedicated workers to the point that there aren't enough people left to carry out the programs.

Authority is defined as the function of deciding preferability and priorities for a group of people. To shrink from deciding is to decide in favor of chaos. Decisions can cover a wide or a narrow range of topics and activities, leaving others to the discretion of individuals. Various decisions can be made by a designated individual or subgroup, by a majority vote, or by consensus. Enforcement can be harshly rigid, gently permissive, or somewhere between those poles, and can vary from topic to topic. In the case of Kalamazoo Youth Ministry, a style of authority and cooperation evolved out of necessity. We had to develop cooperation among ourselves and elicit cooperation from those we served in order to survive and to be effective. May the processes and conceptual frameworks described be useful to the reader and carry with them peace and laughter.

Bobbie Gerber

Chapter One

The Messiah Complex

W hat is the matter with you?" my husband complains. "You have a comfortable home and two lovely daughters. Couldn't you just be my wife and sit back and enjoy life as it comes? No! You've got to have that crumby job where you get paid late half the time. You spend all day in your crumby office and then you're on the phone all evening with somebody who'd as soon slash your tires as look at you. Who appointed you to save the world? Have you got some kind of a Messiah Complex?"

"My job isn't crumby!" I shout at him. "Crumby is doing trivial things all day that aren't a matter of life and death to anybody. Crumby is when nothing in life is more important than whether or not I get my tires slashed. Or my throat, for that matter!" And then I would simmer down and try to explain for the seventieth time. Marlin only complained because he loved me. He put up with a lot, and most of the time he accepted my job in the emergency shelter, even if he didn't always understand. He was right about a couple of things. My office was crumby. The carpeting under my desk chair was worn through and the ceiling looked as if it were going to fall at any moment. And I did have a messiah complex in the sense that I was doing some unselfish things for selfish reasons.

I never had any delusions about saving the world. Jesus didn't tap me on the shoulder and tell me to go into the ministry. There were no visitations of angels whispering that I should work at that emergency shelter. I didn't even have strong feelings about young women with problems until I began doing counseling with them. I meandered into my calling because I'm an odd sort of person who laughs and cries in all the wrong places.

My messiah complex was my response to a dream I must have had twenty or thirty times, a nightmare, actually. The dream taught me that my life isn't really safe anywhere. It made me recognize, in my life prior to ministry, a huge void of substance and meaning. It prompted the decision that I'd rather risk my life for a purpose than to have it snatched away from me for no purpose at all.

In the dream, my home and my thought process are pretty much as they are in real life. Marlin and I live in an ordinary two-story colonial house. There are six others just like it on our street. Marlin is at work. He's an instructor in a community college. Our teenaged daughters are in school. I am at home alone, cleaning the house. In the beginning of the dream a nauseating vividness of textures and odors is my only clue that something terrible is about to happen.

I put the breakfast dishes into the dishwasher and wash the plastic surfaces of the table and counter free of stickiness and crumbs. I scrub the kitchen floor, which is also plastic, grooved to look like cobblestone. Whoever designed it had no sympathy at all for housewives whose task it is to scrape the crud out of those crevices. I don't do a careful job. Floor coverings should all be dirt-colored so that I don't feel guilty about their not being immaculately clean. The trouble with me is that I've always had more respect for dirt than for plastic.

I have a big, noisy vacuum cleaner that masks the sound of the telephone, the doorbell, or anyone entering the house. I've been startled so many times by someone returning home when

I'm running it that I automatically keep looking over my shoulder when it's on. It sucks the sand and fireplace ashes from the orange shag carpeting in the family room. It tears the cat hair off the green olefin upholstery. These synthetic fabrics wear like iron, but a million little fiber fingers grip hair and lint as if their lives depended on it.

I get out a rag and window cleaner and wipe the finger marks off the glass sliding patio door and the dust off the pictures in the living room. They are all black and white wood block prints with haunting images of birds and ladders and faces and crosses. Marlin and I have a friend who is an artist. The prints that fascinate me in his studio late at night after a couple of glasses of wine are not always the easiest pictures to live with.

Finally I spray lemon scented furniture wax on another rag to dust. The bookshelves take the most time. We have too many books and not enough shelves. Marlin accumulates textbooks on economics and accounting, and paperbacks on how to start his own small business and how to get the most from his consumer dollar. I collect trashy novels, multiple volume theological references and commentaries, textbooks on psychology, and knitting patterns. Just for fun, I stick Erica Jong's *Fear of Flying* between the two volumes of Calvin's *Institutes*. That ought to keep the dust from settling!

The conglomeration of furniture in the house is almost as idiosyncratic as the arrangement of books. Marlin and I have divergent tastes and the decor looks like it was designed by a committee. There's a stark Danish end table that my mother got tired of, and a caned rocker that once belonged to Marlin's grandfather. Neither Marlin nor I can pass up a gift or a bargain. Neither of us can bear to discard anything—it might be the exact item we need the very next week. We have a kind of absentminded affection for things just because they've been around for so long.

The routine that is so comfortable and familiar when I'm awake is oppressively monotonous in my dream. My movements seem like those of a macabre ritual that can't be altered or interrupted.

The smells of ammonia and furniture wax remind me of a sultry August day when I was eleven years old. My mother and I had cleaned the whole house and everything was spotless. A late afternoon thunderstorm came up, and with it a stunning crash of lightning. We could smell the ozone, but couldn't see any damage, even upstairs or in the attic. My mother led my sister and me by the hands into the living room. "I think we should sit down," she said, "and thank God that the lightning didn't strike our house and cause a fire." We bowed our heads and smelled smoke.

The house didn't burn to the ground, but the inside was pretty thoroughly ruined. I lost that day my childlike faith that God would protect me individually from catastrophe. Bad things could happen to me as well as anybody else.

In my dream I move upstairs in my house. Ever since the fire I've felt as if I were tempting fate if I had the whole house clean at the same time. I decide against cleaning my daughters' rooms. What's the point of having a room of one's own if one's mother cleans it!

When I moved out of the college dormitory into my husband's apartment as a young bride, I developed the habit of grooming myself and cleaning the bathroom in one operation. In the dream, as in real life, I take off all of my clothes and begin by straightening up the clutter on the bathroom counter. Then I shower and begin scrubbing the tub and the tile around it. The doors are locked, the house is quiet. Naked in the steamy warmth of the bathroom, I become introspective and philosophical. Some of my better ideas about life are more or less loosely associated with scrubbing mildew out of the tile grout.

Does God in Heaven really care about mildew? Probably. The stuff is made up of little plants that have the remarkable ability to thrive on soap scum and moisture in the air. Do they feel terror and anguish as their little cells are ripped apart with detergent and scrub brush? Do their souls weep as the stain of their existence is obliterated with bleach? Maybe. But what passes for civilization, not to mention hygiene, depends upon controlling little creatures like this. If I leave them long enough, they'll eat away the grout and the tiles will fall off the wall.

If the tile has to be cleaned, does God in Heaven care how much I hate doing it? Probably. Rationally, I have three options. I can clean it and resent it, and stain my relationships with Marlin and the girls. But resentment eats away the mortar of our love and leaves a foul-smelling stain in our life together. The second choice would be to ask somebody else to clean it. Marlin would probably be willing to take his turn, but he always un-clogs the drains and it doesn't seem quite fair. The girls take long showers, luxuriously oblivious to the tile and porcelain. They come downstairs, humming tunes, confident and expect-ant, smelling like lilacs, and looking so wholesomely gorgeous they make my teeth itch. Do I want to ask at such a moment if they've wiped out the shower stall, or just say, "Wow, you look terrific!"? I prefer the latter. My third option is to learn not to hate it.

It's just at the moment in my dream when I am on the verge of discovering the ultimate meaning of love and mildew. The bathroom door bursts open. I freeze in the chilly draft. As I slowly look up, I see a bluejeaned figure in a ski mask. I have no idea how he got in. After the first shocked gasp, I force myself to go limp. The nightmare projector goes into slow motion. The intruder grabs me across the shoulder and chest, brandishes a knife at my throat, and says, "Don't scream."

I take a deep breath and whisper, "Don't worry, I won't. What do you want?"

"Whatever I can get," he answers.

I take another deep breath and relax my arm and shoulder muscles so that his grip is less painful. I've had this dream so many times I'm getting good at it. When I first began having it, I always panicked and got my throat slashed right there in the bathroom.

"Listen," I say, "I can't fight my way out of a paper bag, and I can't run very fast, either. Why don't you let go of me, and I'll go put on a bathrobe and we'll go downstairs and I'll make you a cup of coffee."

"I didn't break in here for a goddamn cup of coffee!" he says gruffly. "What are you trying to pull?"

"I'm not trying to pull anything," I reply. "It's just that we are both in an embarrassing, uncomfortable situation, and I propose that we simply talk it over like two civilized human beings." Strange as things can be in dreams, we do just that.

Over coffee, with the ski mask still in place, he tells me that he is a heroin addict and needs a fix. He wants anything in the house that can be sold. Since I have a degree in counseling, it occurs to me to suggest that he obtain treatment for his habit. On second thought, I offer him half a bottle of tranquilizers and some pain pills containing codeine from the medicine cabinet. I hope he'll take the lot of them on the spot, and mellow out. He puts the pill bottles in his pocket.

I explain to him that he is welcome to the silverware, but I just cleaned the house and would appreciate it if he didn't make too much of a mess. I am very helpful. There was a portable radio and a pocket calculator on the desk. The dishes are too much trouble to pack, and the artwork is too easy to trace. I help him unfasten the wires on the television and the stereo. The insurance won't cover the replacement of these things, but I'll get more for them than if I had a garage sale. It's almost fun.

When we've gathered up everything I can think of, including the money in my purse, the situation again becomes grim. It occurs to me and to him at the same time that as he carries the loot out the front door, I could run out the back. I suggest that we stay close together, and I help him carry everything out. But I'd have the description and license number of his van. I could go into a closet and he could bar the door with a chair. He won't trust it unless I'm bound hand and foot. Quickly I calculate that my chances of survival are better if I cooperate. He ties my wrists and ankles together with the sash of my bathrobe.

I'm never quite able to exert enough conscious control over the dream to make the intruder leave me tied up until the kids get home from school. Bound, helpless, and for all practical purposes naked, I am stabbed and raped. I hold with all my tenacious rationality to the notion that I'll be hurt less if I don't struggle. Panic roars in my ears like a giant vacuum cleaner and sucks away the synthetic fibers of my self-control. I scream and feel myself writhe in warm, slippery blood. Struggling makes matters worse, but I can't stop doing it. At the height of my anguish and terror, I lose consciousness, and regain it only long enough to pray, "God help me get into that closet so the kids won't see me like this when they walk in the door."

I put no stock whatsoever in even such a vivid and recurring dream as a premonition. I can handle risk in real life when I'm awake. The odds against my getting stabbed and raped in my own home are about as slim as the odds against the house I live in being struck by lightning. After I've insisted upon lightning rods for the house, I figure I've done everything I can to prevent it and don't worry about it any more. When I'm at home alone I lock the doors. When I go out alone at night, I am alert and cautious, especially in a high-crime neighborhood. If I have to walk through a poorly lighted, isolated place, I hold my keys in my fist so they stick out through my fingers like brass knuckles. I doubt that someone who's squeamish about the weeping soul of mildew would be capable of tearing off someone's face with a set of keys. The advantage is psychological. The keys are like the lightning rods; they keep me from feeling afraid. As a result, my gait and posture are not those of a likely victim.

It's not the real-life possibility of being raped and stabbed that bothers me about the dream. It's the meaninglessness of it all. It's why it might possibly happen. I can think of three factors contributing to the potential of my being killed in the way I imagine while I'm at home alone. The first is that I am economically privileged. The second is that rage and violence are a fact of life in our society. The third is that I am a woman.

With regard to the first factor, you will remember that the intruder initially wanted to rob me. In his mind, I was one of the "haves," and he was one of the "have-nots." To some extent I would have been a victim of the uneven distribution of wealth in the world. Heaven knows I acknowledge my fair share of guilt about that!

When I was eighteen years old, I went to Mexico with several other college students to see the sights and to work at a little mission in the mountains of the northern province of Chihuahua. We visited a poor family and took them some baby clothes and some food. They had two babies, twins, a boy and a girl eight months old. The babies weighed only about eight pounds each. Because they'd been in incubators, the mother's milk was unavailable. Infant formula was expensive and there were other children to feed, so the mother added water to it. Sterilizing anything in the little adobe hut was impossible. What happens to tourists who aren't used to the water also happens to babies. They get dysentery.

The little girl seemed healthier and more alert than the little boy. Most of the group fussed over her. I went to the little boy. His face was thin and wrinkled, his eyes wide. His abdomen was distended and he looked like an old man. His arms and legs were only a little thicker than my thumbs. I carefully picked him up. I had never held a small baby before, and I was afraid his head would wobble around or that he might wriggle out of my arms. He was very limp and hardly moved. The light weight of his body was ghostly. I wished I could nurse him at my own breast, and felt sadder than I've ever felt before or since in my whole life. I held him until it was time to leave, then kissed him on the top of his head and laid him back down in his bed. His name, like that of many Mexican boys, was Jèsus.

At that time my father was making a living and paying my college expenses by storing hundreds of thousands of bushels of corn. The United States government had purchased the corn and paid for its storage in warehouses in order to support farm prices. If grain were too cheap, modern mechanized farming would not be a viable economic enterprise. Without mechanization, not enough food could be produced. My father was not an ogre, hoarding food from the starving masses. He was a good man, a conscientious Mennonite. He thought of himself as being like Joseph in the Bible, who built warehouses in Egypt to ensure food against a famine. He sent money to organizations that provided hunger relief in other parts of the world.

Growing up in a central Illinois farming community in the fifties, I had never thought of this field corn as food. Corn was feed for animals so that we could have marbled steak and juicy hamburgers. Nowadays Mexican restaurants are almost as common as hamburger stands once were, and everybody knows that corn can be ground into flour and made into tortillas and wrapped around beans. The combination is a complete protein which can keep people from starving, and the stuff tastes good. This was an amazing realization for a midwestern kid in 1960.

Being only eighteen years old, I could not reconcile the two experiences of that starving baby and those huge buildings full of corn. I knew that there were millions of starving babies all over the world. I couldn't love millions of babies, but only one at a time. If I were to spend my whole life taking care of such children, I might have been able to save twenty or forty or a few hundred. Would they then have grown up and had babies of their own who would starve? When you're eighteen and idealistic, it's not enough to save a few starving babies, and one is too many.

In September, the missionaries who'd hosted the students in Mexico mentioned in a letter that the little boy twin had died. I went out and bought a crucifix and hung it in my room in the college dormitory. Under it I taped a lettered sign that read, " Jèsus died for your sins in Cuatèmoc, Chihuahua, on August 18, 1960, of infantile dysentery and malnutrition."

That was more than twenty years ago, the self-torturing blasphemy of a schoolgirl. But even as I write about it I still feel like I have a toothache in my chest and want to cry. My sense of the presence of Christ in the world today is still inextricably entwined with the memory of that weightless, withered body and those suffering, innocent eyes.

Marlin and I still give money to the hunger relief organizations. Most of the time I'm a vegetarian, but I don't like to make a fuss about it when I'm invited to somebody's house for dinner. I'm still middle class, and still benefiting from the liberal arts education paid for by my father storing government surplus corn. I couldn't help having been born into my family any more than that baby could help having been born into his. I had been no better able to change my class and economic status than his family had been to change theirs. Both the baby and I in my nightmare are casualties of economic inequity. For me to die because I'm middle class would be as meaningless and useless as his dying of starvation.

Economics is a crumby reason to die, and no more substantial as a reason to live. Money can make life a lot more pleasant and comfortable, but for me, it doesn't give life meaning. The nightmare reveals how I feel about it. There I was in my comfortable isolation, surrounded by so many worldly goods I didn't appreciate any of them. Everything I cleaned was synthetic and plastic. The dirt was at least an authentic substance. I was willing to give away anything I owned as soon as my life was threatened. To devote my life primarily or exclusively to acquiring and maintaining lifeless objects doesn't make sense to me. I needed a purpose beyond my own comfort, more important than my own existence. Working in a ministry that provided food and care for people who were destitute provided that kind of purpose. Then my work, my relationships and even possessions could be organized into a coherent pattern around that purpose. To me, at least, the ideal made sense.

I dislike the idea of dying as a helpless victim of rage as much as I dislike the idea of dying because of economic privilege. As a counselor in the shelter, I listened to bitter stories of violence in childhood told by dozens of young people, any of whom could have been the figure in the ski mask. I learned how someone could become angry enough to kill. Of course not all people who were abused as children become murderers. Nor do all murderers have this kind of background. But about eighty percent of individuals convicted of violent crimes were abused as children, according to various surveys of prisoners. If not a direct cause, child abuse is a factor in increasing the potential for an act such as murder.

Imagine the fellow as a small child. His mother is young and alone, and has emotional and economic problems. She has little patience, and spanks her baby when he cries or whines. From time to time, one of her boyfriends moves in with her. When he's drunk, his idea of how to shut up a kid is to throw him bodily against a wall. Maybe the neighbors call the police, and the child enters the revolving door of foster homes and institutions.

A little boy like this is taught very early that he's not supposed to cry. The more abusive his environment, the more likely he is to be punished for it. If he cries, he's "a sissy." The tears and sobs he's not allowed to shed come to be identified with that which is feminine. Effeminacy begets punishment; he's learned that lesson! Insofar as murder can be thought of as suicide projected on someone else, it's a way of killing the part of himself that's "a sissy."

A woman may also remind him of his mother, from whom he needed comfort and love and didn't get it. The attention he was most likely to get from her was a whack across the face. Anger filled the void of love, violence the void of affection. Anger and violence are the only responses to need and pain he's ever received. When love is supplanted by rage, there is no rage equal to that reserved for the first love object, the mother. His feelings toward her, however, are too mixed with need to permit him to kill her and are buried far below the surface of his consciousness. So he takes out his rage on someone who reminds him of her by virtue of being the same gender, a woman.

The rage factor is closely connected with the factor of being a woman. Because I was a woman he didn't expect me to be able to defend myself effectively. He expected me to panic and submit. It made absolutely no difference that everything I did was consistent with the Sermon on the Mount. It made absolutely no difference that I deeply believe in nonviolence as a principle, the little trick with the keyring notwithstanding. If I were killed

in the manner of the dream, the coffee cups would lead ev
body else to think that the assailant was someone I had let
the house. It would never occur to anyone that I was surpr
while doing the household task which, for me, required the m;on
real love. It would never occur to anyone that, even wh f
threatened, I would behave hospitably to a stranger and attemp.
to negotiate with him as a human being. My nudity in the shreds
of my housecoat would leave the impression that I had an illicit
lover. The very evidence of my love would look like the stain
of adultery.

That's not the kind of stain I want my life to leave, not on my
family and friends, nor even on strangers who might read about
my death in the newspaper. In a way, wanting to be remembered for anything is self-serving, and in that way I do have a
messiah complex. It is also true that I was dissatisfied with a life
that served only my own comfort and self-perpetuation, that I
longed for a purpose beyond my own existence. "The chief end
of man," according to the Westminster Catechism, "is to glorify
God and to enjoy Him forever." Glory, as the term is used in
the Fourth Gospel, is a visual phenomenon, something that was
seen, through which the Messiah was recognized. To glorify
God, then, is to weave the tapestry of one's life in such a way
that the identity of the Messiah can be recognized through it.
Seeking to do this, albeit in fear and trembling, is salvation from
the tyranny of human opinion. The endeavor toward this end
by serving others is ministry whether one is ordained or not.

I felt an intense urge toward ministry, almost a physical desire, after the experience with the baby in Mexico. I expressed
that urge by marrying Marlin and having babies of my own.
When my children were no longer babies and I was looking for
a career, I seriously considered going to seminary. The nearest
seminary, however, was sixty miles away. I was reluctant to
spend long periods of time away from my husband and daughters and have not regretted that decision. Besides that, in 1972
I'd never laid eyes on an ordained woman minister, and the
probability of my ever getting a job within commuting distance

of Kalamazoo, where I lived, seemed very slim indeed. I undertook, instead, a master's degree in counseling with a few religion courses on the side from a local university.

As it turned out, Kalamazoo already had so many counselors that my chances of being hired as a counselor right after graduate school, with no experience, weren't much better than my chances of being hired as a minister. In order to get the necessary experience, I began looking for an organization that would use my services as a volunteer.

Through a friend, who was also seeking employment as a counselor, I heard of Kalamazoo Youth Ministry. It was a small organization that offered emergency shelter to teenaged runaways and drug users. The ministry operated two rundown houses in a rundown neighborhood with a shoestring budget and half enough staff. My friend and I were both drawn by the need for our services there, but she was dissuaded from working there by the organization's religious emphasis. She was offended that in her initial interview she was queried more about her Christian conviction than her professional qualifications. I was terrified of tough adolescents, as evidenced in my nightmare, and had no faith in the effectiveness of my meager counseling skills to save my neck, let alone help them. If, however, the primary requirement was religious commitment, I felt as though I could handle just about anything.

I found at the ministry the finest group of dedicated Christians I ever expect to meet anywhere. I think initially most of them were as afraid that I would disapprove of them as I was that they would disapprove of me. They thought of me as an intellectual because I had spent so many years in school and liked to use words to understand and solve problems. They thought of me as a liberal because I used the psychological jargon of counseling texts more than I quoted from the Bible. They thought of me as an egotist because of my middle class accoutrements and my self-consciousness. Still, they welcomed me with open arms. I knew I had found a home there when I was introduced as "a Presbyterian elder who has a degree in counseling" rather than vice versa. They were so desperately in need of any kind of help that they encouraged me to do any-thing I was foolhardy enough to try.

Within a few weeks I became so intrigued with the work I was allowed to do, and so deeply satisfied with being needed and appreciated, that I gave up looking for a paying job. The friend who had directed me to the ministry in the first place was horrified. "Do you mean to tell me," she exclaimed, "that you're going to give away the best years of your life?" I only gave away one or two days a week for two and a half years before I was hired to work for the ministry full time. The nearly seven years I devoted to the ministry were the best years of my life, so far anyway.

They were tiring, gruesome, harrowing years when death was more than a fantasy. They were funny, exciting, fascinating years, full of irony and purpose and meaning. I loved and laughed and learned, and I got mad and frustrated and de-pressed. And I was no longer afraid of dying.

Shortly after I began my work, I was talking with a minister whose interpretation of the Scriptures was literal and legalistic. He was trying to frighten me into his way of thinking when he asked, "What would you do if you were to meet your maker right now?"

"I would hope," I replied, "that I would do what any Chris-tian in his or her right mind would do under the circumstances. That is to fall on my face and beg for mercy."

That wasn't what he had in mind. "How would you justify yourself to Jesus?" he pressed. "How would you give account for the life He gave you? Do you know right now that He'd let you into heaven?"

"Well, not for sure," I answered. "But I've been spending quite a bit of time lately feeding the hungry, providing shelter for strangers, and visiting folks in mental hospitals and in jail. I've never run across any who were naked so I could clothe them, but I knit a lot of mittens for people with cold hands. Jesus may have some bones to pick with me about my pride and self-indulgence, but I've got it in black and white that He's going to recognize me. He said that when we've done those kinds of things for the least of these, brother, we've done them for Him."

I didn't usually think in literal terms about getting into heaven. I remembered, thinking about the conversation later, that we're not going to be included in the Kingdom because of anything we do or don't do. We are included because of Christ's grace and mercy.

Much worse for me than the prospect of death itself was the prospect of a meaningless death. My death as a helpless casualty of economics and rage against women would have been as meaningless as a life spent tending my possessions and pacifying other people. Ministry gave me an alternative to my nightmare of waiting in my semi-clean house to become a victim. I was out in the dirty, real world, doing battle with its chaos firsthand. I could invest my life in showing concrete evidence of love to people who had never known how it felt. I could offer my potential murderer access to the ultimate Sacrifice which could really heal him.

I figured that I was going to die sooner or later in any case, so I might as well exit with pizazz. Pizazz is the exhilarating realization that if I were to die within the next few minutes, my life had been well spent. Pizazz is the coming together of past and present, of some forgotten experience being demanded by the situation and used in God's scheme for the ministry. Pizazz is the little glimpses of underlying meaning in the fabric of my daily life. Pizazz is the polar opposite of crumby.

There are people who work in shelter ministry whose motivations are much less selfish than mine. I'll introduce people in subsequent chapters who devoted their lives to the ministry much more fully than I did. I want to make clear the contrast between those people and me.

It is not essential, however, that the motivation of everyone involved in such a ministry be absolutely pure. It doesn't matter that some people are initially motivated by the need to be needed, others to justify their existence, and still others to do

something interesting. That services are provided and that people are treated well are more important than the purity of an
individual's motivation to do the work. Unselfishness takes
practice. It is essential that we are totally honest before God
about our motivation and the benefits we derive from helping
people. Otherwise the ministry can become self-serving in ways
that are detrimental to the people being served.

The more honest we are, the more we see that the stain of
our selfishness permeates everything that we do. The more we
try to avoid it, the more it creeps up on us. It is a byproduct of
our life processes, egocentric creatures that we are. May God
bleach our stains with His mercy so the glory of His Kingdom
may be seen.

※ | *Chapter Two*

Saints or Fools

Hospitality and lodging for strangers has been part of the Judeo-Christian tradition from the earliest times. In the Pentateuch the Israelites were commanded to offer shelter because they "were strangers in the land of Egypt." In the New Testament, the Gospels mention it several times. The best-known parable about "the least of these" is found toward the end of Matthew 25. Matthew 22:2 ff. and Luke 14:12 ff. are parables of feasts in which the guests are invited from the highways and byways and include the poor, the lame and the blind. One of the standards listed repeatedly in the epistles for both male and female Christians is hospitality.

Medieval monasteries, convents, and even cathedrals offered lodging for widows, for the poor, the blind, and the crippled. In more recent times, the Salvation Army, the Gospel Missions, the YWCA and YMCA have responded to the need for shelter in America. The Catholic Worker movement has articulated the argument for shelter for over fifty years, and their houses of hospitality remain in operation in various parts of the country. In Europe during the Second World War, Christians sheltered and hid Jews and others who were in danger, at tremendous risk to themselves. Corrie Ten Boom's *The Hiding Place* tells some of those stories. Foreign mission endeavors of American churches have been directed toward refugees of war and famines in many parts of the world. Groups of Christians scattered throughout the country, living separately or in community, make a practice of taking strangers into their homes for varying lengths of time.

Kalamazoo Youth Ministry did not begin with the intention of offering shelter. The organization was the brainchild of a young dentist, Dr. Robert Hosack, his wife, Sally, and their friends, Ron and Marty Snyder. Their vision of offering hospitality was to start a coffee house.

During the late sixties, the hippie movement was in full swing in the midwest. Teenagers, even some from good homes, were rebelling against the established authority, dropping out of school, and turning to the use of drugs. Though it was the voluntary participation of middle-class kids that really aroused the concern of the community, the majority fled from abusive homes and tragic childhoods into the dangerous, underground drug culture. They stole and fought in order to survive, and experimented with sex and drugs for fun. The drugs were magical, horrible substances that no one, including the individuals who were using them, knew very much about. Overdoses and drug induced psychotic episodes were common occurrences. The whole phenomenon was very frightening.

The initial reactions of most parents, teachers, churchgoers, social workers, and police were generally punitive. Only a handful of people nationwide were willing to reach out to the kids, to take to the streets and listen to what they had to say and try to help. Dave Wilkerson in Harlem was beginning the work that became widely known in his book *The Cross and the Switchblade*. Groups pejoratively known as "Jesus freaks" were spreading through the youth culture in California. With aggressive tactics and Christian rock music, they tried to convert everyone they encountered. Street ministry at the time was a radical.

A minister named Larry Love, who had trained with Billy Graham, was serving as pastor of First Reformed Church in downtown Kalamazoo. Despite widespread misgivings, he began a program to get the youth off the streets and into the basement of his church. The Hosacks and the Snyders helped out. The program was short-lived, but Bob and Sally were left with what they called "a burden on their hearts for the kids who were turned off by the established churches." Ron Snyder was a social worker at Kalamazoo Child Guidance Clinic. He and his wife, Marty, had great compassion for young people. Bob had a gift for starting and organizing projects, and began talking with the Snyders and other friends about his idea for a Christian coffee house.

Coffee houses and drop-in centers for youth were already in operation in various cities and towns across the nation. People were ready to offer enthusiastic support for any plan that sounded promising for dealing with the awesome problem of alienated youth. After months of research, planning, and praying, Bob and Sally began to look for a storefront location in which to place their dream. They searched for months, but none was available at a price their group could afford. They found, instead, a little old house tucked back away from the street in a residential area on the outskirts of the business district. Its most obvious advantage was that it could be leased for seventy-five dollars a month.

In the fall of 1970, proposals were written, financial statements prepared, and a board of directors was assembled for a nonprofit corporation to be called Kalamazoo Youth Ministry. Most of the money came from board members themselves, who were primarily business and professional men, and friends of Bob and Ron. Campus clergy were also interested. A Missionary Bible Church handled the money prior to incorporation so that contributions would be tax deductible.

The original board of directors drew up a statement of faith for their coffee house ministry. They believed in the infallible authority of the Bible, the Trinity, the deity of Christ, salvation, the resurrection of souls, and the spiritual unity of all believers in Christ.

The primary goal of the coffee house was "to communicate

the Gospel of Jesus Christ to unchurched young people." One of the basic principles was "Love is not only something you FEEL; it is something you DO." The earliest official proposal quoted 1 Corinthians 9:20–21 from the Living New Testament.

> When I am with the Jews, I seem as one of them so that they will listen to the Gospel and I can win them to Christ. When I am with the Gentiles who follow Jewish customs and ceremonies I don't argue, even though I don't agree, because I want to help them. When with the heathen I agree with them as much as I can, except of course that I must always do what is right as a Christian. And so, by agreeing, I can win their confidence and help them too.

The idea was not to "beat people over the head with the Bible," but to win them over with love. Although the documents containing these statements were lost for several years, their influence could be heard and felt through the many changes that took place.

The board also hired a director for the coffee house, who recruited and trained the original volunteer staff. There were twelve young men and women on the staff, ranging in age from seventeen to twenty-three. Some were former drug users. Others came from sheltered Christian homes and schools, and were completely naive about the drug scene. They were selected for such attributes as personal integrity, tact, listening ability, loyalty, ability to follow instructions, flexibility, sensitivity, diligence, perseverance, financial responsibility, and creativity. They were asked how and when Jesus became personal to them, and how they were cultivating their spiritual lives. How they related to Christians who were different from themselves and to people of other racial and ethnic groups was also an issue. They were asked for a personal response to the statement: "Being a staff member at the coffee house will require a total commitment to that ministry." They were variously called "Jesus People" and "enthusiastic young Christians."

Staff training took the form of an intensive retreat, which emphasized sensitivity to others and a growing relationship with Christ.

The board and staff together set about refurbishing the little house they had leased, which came to be known as The Open Door. The building itself seemed to rebel against paint and wallpaper, causing layer after layer to blister and peel. Nails fell out of the woodwork like rotten teeth. Plaster came loose like clumps of hair. Windows and ceilings sagged and leaked. Smoke, grime, and mildew clung like a grey beard. The house was a century-old derelict, held together mainly by unrelenting efforts to cheer it up.

Fortunately, dilapidation was high fashion in the youth culture of that era. With a great investment of energy and imagination, the volunteers created a usable little coffee house. They decorated two rooms with posters and colored lights, and collected old furniture and telephone cable spools for whatever their prospective customers might want to do. They outfitted a narrow room at the rear of the house with a rugged, ceiling-high cross, and painted its windows for a chapel. They blocked off the kitchen so that coffee and food served from it would be safe from contamination with drugs. Two rooms upstairs became an office and a counseling room. The cold, uneven floor and walls of the basement were covered with carpeting so that the rooms could be used for group discussions and staff meetings. Four evenings a week were designated for drop-ins.

There was amazingly little resistance from the neighborhood to having a coffee house or drop-in center there. Ranney Street, where The Open Door was located, was only a block long, and connected two major thoroughfares. Many of the houses had already been divided into cheap apartments for tenants of an age and economic category to pass for students. Drug traffic, crime, and rowdiness were already serious problems for older residents and businessmen on the main streets. The staff and board members walked the streets and talked to everyone, young and old, letting people know that their primary goal was to share Jesus' love. Even if it sounded a little crazy, it was an improvement over what was already going on in the neighborhood.

By Halloween, The Open Door was ready to be open. It happened that a local church youth group planned a hunger walk on that day, a forerunner to the marathons in which participants solicit pledges of donations for hunger relief based on the number of miles walked. The walk was followed by a meal, at which the walkers had a choice between rice, in keeping with the theme, or a generous meal of hot dogs. Nearly everyone chose the rice. That evening the pastor was left with several hundred hot dogs he didn't know what to do with. He called someone from The Open Door and asked if the food could be used.

Somebody borrowed a pickup truck, and loaded up the hot dogs. As goblins and demons filled the streets at dusk, the little band of Jesus People set out to give away their hot dogs and invite people to come to The Open Door. They threw down the gauntlet of love with an enormous Halloween party!

About the time The Open Door was officially opened, a staff member named Karla Meana was looking for an apartment. She was a student and had very little money. It seemed like a good idea for her to move into The Open Door to provide maintenance and security in lieu of rent. Karla was the composer of the lovely ballad, "Emmaus Road." Seven stanzas of the song chronicled events in Jesus' life. The first and last stanza read:

> "Well, my teacher, he's mighty fine.
> He changed water into wine.
> Taught me what it meant to give,
> Even died that I might live."

Within a couple of weeks the weather turned cold. Hundreds of young people were coming to The Open Door for drop-ins. They were loading the coffee with sugar because they had nothing to eat. They were sleeping on the porch because they had no place else to go. Karla could not say to them, "I love you, but go away during my suppertime." She could not say, "I love you, but you can't sleep on my porch." So she began to feed people, Heaven only knows how. She began to invite them inside to sleep on couches or, in the slang of that era, to crash on the floor. She didn't have much to offer, but what she had was better than the wet, cold ground.

It was Karla who quietly involved the youth ministry in shelter. Another staff member, Jane Harmon, moved in to help her. The "crashers" were guests in their home. Board members and other staff also took into their own homes young people who needed housing and love. Shelter continued unofficially for months before a proposal which listed it as one of the services the ministry provided was formally adopted by the board.

By March of 1971, a number of changes had taken place. Karla and Jane moved out of The Open Door, and were replaced by Dan Stoepker and his teenaged foster son. Dan was on the original staff, a recent college graduate, and the first single person in the state of Michigan to become a licensed foster parent. The first director of the youth ministry resigned, and his work was taken over temporarily by a board member who also had a full time supervisory job in a factory. The cash balance on hand was ninety-one cents.

The community's demands for drug-abuse treatment were practically overwhelming. The telephone rang around the clock. Worried parents called and asked for information about missing sons and daughters. Usually the staff had not seen them, and could only assure the parents The Open Door was available and ready to help if the child should turn up. The staff was always truthful with both parents and young people and gave neither information without the other knowing it. The criteria for sharing information were that it was shared in love, and not destructive to either party. The staff prayed for the families, and called the parents again later. Sometimes they had news. Sometimes they could only say that they were still keeping an eye out for the son or daughter and praying.

The young people were calling to ask for help with their problems: romantic breakups, the temptation to commit suicide, and bad experiences with drugs. These telephone counseling sessions sometimes went on for hours.

Barbie was a new volunteer. She was a student, and came from a solid Christian Reformed home against which she never felt the need to rebel. She was enthusiastic, loving, and innocent. One night when she was giving Dan a break from answering the phone, the police called. They needed a place to leave a man who was recovering from an overdose of some unknown drug. He had been examined in the hospital emergency room, and just needed someone to stay with him until the effect of the drug wore off. Such calls were not unusual at The Open Door, and Barbie agreed to take care of him.

The police brought the man into The Open Door on a stretcher and dumped him on a couch. The man was thrashing around, moaning, and talking crazy. Barbie ran upstairs to try to wake Dan, but he was too exhausted to help. She returned to the man and tried to soothe him as best she could. He began to say, "I've got to piss! I've got to piss!" so she offered to help him into the bathroom. The minute he was off the couch he started putting his hands all over her. Terrified, she tried once more to rouse Dan, who was for all practical purposes unconscious. When she came back downstairs, she found the man in the bathroom, partly undressed and soaking wet. Somehow, she pulled up his pants and led him back to the couch. Then she sat down with her Bible and began to read aloud from the Gospel of John. Reading had a calming effect on both Barbie and the drug victim, and that was how she passed the night.

There was a street gang that hung around The Open Door in the early days. They often disrupted chapel services and harassed both staff and visitors as they left at night. One night during chapel, a fight broke out in the parking lot. It was a bloody fight with chains and knives, and people were getting hurt. Dan, who was leading the chapel service, charged out the door into the middle of the fray, yelling God knows what at the top of his lungs. The frightened worshipers inside, fearful that Dan would be killed, joined hands and stormed Heaven's gates for his safety. The fight broke up instantly, and the gang slowly retreated, never to cause serious trouble again. Those who needed medical treatment were taken to the hospital, and Dan returned safe to the loving arms of his friends.

Many of the actions of the early staff seem foolhardy in retrospect. They subjected themselves to serious danger and tremendous abuse. Their parents were frantic about their safety. There was no prestige or personal glory in working at The Open Door. The hours were long and hard, the demands insurmountable, and they weren't even getting paid for it. Still, they never hesitated for a moment to do anything they felt called upon to do to serve God and to love people. Their courage and commitment provided a standard of saintliness which inspired those of us who arrived on the scene in later years. Their faith sustained them beyond the limits of normal human endurance. Their prayers were answered, and they were protected from harm even on the few occasions when their actions were genuinely foolish.

Once a young staff member drove a couple of fellows home in her parents' car after drop-in. They made a few brief stops under the pretext of seeing friends en route. Money changed hands, but the innocent driver did not realize until later that she had provided transportation for a narcotics deal. If violence had erupted, as it can in illicit dealings, she might have been hurt or killed. If they had been caught, she almost certainly would have been arrested.

The staff learned not to take unnecessary risks or to allow themselves to be used as pawns in the dope business. They would not, however, have hesitated to go to jail if that were an unavoidable consequence of associating with drug users. A grand jury investigation into drug traffic in Kalamazoo began that spring. Undercover narcotics agents frequented the drop-ins. If the agents had found evidence that drugs were being used and sold on the premises, staff members could have been called into court to testify. The staff members would not have lied, but neither would they have betrayed confidences. They could have been charged with contempt of court.

The staff was less worried about going to jail than about narcotics agents who might scare away people who needed help. Representatives from the youth ministry and from other fledgling drug treatment agencies sat down with officials to talk. The latter were concerned that drug treatment facilities would become major centers of drug trading if people were safe there from arrest and subpoena. They acknowledged that drug counseling did not require knowledge of where the drugs came from. The staff made a practice of keeping very few records, not writing down anything that could be taken as evidence.

Clearly, drug traffic at The Open Door had to be curtailed. The staff was too overworked and outnumbered to police it. After they had prayed about it, they took aside a few key people and explained the situation. If they wanted to get rid of the "narcs," they would have to get rid of the drugs. If they didn't want The Open Door to lose its tenuous base of support and have to close down, the street people would have to cooperate in keeping drugs off the premises. It worked. Although the effects of drugs were still very much in evidence, possession was limited to the occasional marijuana joint smoked in the chapel or parking lot, or the little cache of pills in someone's pocket. These were fairly easy for the staff to confront if they had the general support of the people who came for drop-in.

During this time, the board and staff were distinguishable from each other only by age and official voting privileges. They met together for board meetings at 6:30 A.M. in a restaurant for breakfast. Week after week the meetings went on virtually every Wednesday morning until problems were resolved and business was completed. They worked together at The Open Door and prayed and discussed their work before and after drop-in hours. They had potluck meals together. Everyone participated in policy discussions, everyone took turns fulfilling speaking engagements in the community, and everyone worked at raising money and personally gave as much as he or she could.

They saw a need for hospitality, and concerned themselves with keeping the house open for friendship, dialogue, food, and shelter in an atmosphere of genuine love. They turned their love into acts of helping. They did what they could for people, and directed those who needed more extensive services to the other organizations that could provide them. They stood by people throughout their time of need. They were concerned, finally, with communication between parents and children, institutions and individuals, teachers and students, God and humanity. Their mission involved them in communication with and among various churches and other parts of the Body of Christ.

The people who visited The Open Door for drop-in were considered the dregs of society. Nobody else wanted to be around the dirty hippie with long hair or the pregnant teenager who took drugs. At The Open Door they were welcome. They were greeted with smiles and called by name. They were invited to talk to people who really listened and cared what happened to them. Drop-ins, worship services and Bible studies gave them something to do with their time, and the music was enthusiastic and enjoyable.

As summer approached, energy and imagination ran high. Churches, Parent-Teacher Associations, schools, and clubs were requesting programs and drug education. Warmer weather encouraged street work, which meant walking around talking to people in the parks and shopping districts. The staff felt the need to visit people in homes, in hospitals, and in jail. Suggestions were made for arts and crafts programs, sports activities, guitar lessons, concerts, picnics, beach parties and weekend retreats.

In order to do this, the staff needed the economic freedom to put in more time. The board of directors decided to rent two apartments for the summer and to pay the staff people ten dollars a week toward their subsistence. Under this agreement, six more-than-full-time staff members cost the organization only about $400 a month. Some of them solicited their own support from churches or friends. Devotion and commitment make an unsurpassable bargain!

A young Reformed pastor, just out of seminary, came on the scene as director of the ministry in the spring of 1971. His name was Bernie Brower. His job was to coordinate the aforementioned activities, to provide spiritual leadership, to raise funds, and to do everything that everyone else did besides. Bernie was an understanding, caring man with tremendous energy. That first summer was an exciting and purposeful time, unforgettable for those involved.

In the fall, the staff members rented their own apartments just a couple of blocks from The Open Door. Although they had to return to school or find other jobs to support themselves, they remained intimately involved with the ministry.

As the scope of the ministry widened and the work expanded, more room was needed. One idea was to lease or purchase a small farm and go into residential treatment of drug abusers in a more healthy environment. This turned out to be too expensive.

In January of 1972, the owner of The Open Door sold the property to another landlord without even giving the ministry a chance to buy it. The new owner came and inspected the property, and informed Bernie that he had extensive plans for renovation. This would be impossible with The Open Door in operation, so the ministry would have to vacate the premises by April 1. The Open Door was firmly established and the program was in full swing. Funds were extremely low. Starting from scratch in a new location seemed impossible. The saints prayed.

Only a few days later, a large black Cadillac pulled into the driveway. The driver came to the door and asked to speak with the person in charge. He explained to Bernie that he was working for a person who wished to remain anonymous, and his job was to give away this individual's money. He and his employer had taken note of The Open Door, liked the work the people there were doing, and wanted to ensure that it would continue. He handed Bernie a business card, and instructed him to prepare a statement of how much money was needed and the purposes for which it would be used.

The entire board and staff were stunned. They were accustomed to their prayers being answered, but not as dramatically as this! The parcel of land on which The Open Door was situated included the parking lot, a large duplex adjacent to The Open Door, and a little yard behind the duplex. The new owner was willing to part with the property for $18,000. A land contract could be arranged with a down payment of $5,000. Though both houses were in poor repair, this was the property the ministry wanted. The anonymous benefactor provided the down payment and several thousand dollars for renovation.

The black Cadilac story was told and retold among the staff and board for years after that. When fund shortages became desperate and paychecks were late and the telephones were about to be disconnected, the work always went on as if there were a black Cadillac just around the corner. Along with indefatigable hope, the story perpetuated a casual attitude toward fundraising, which may have been one reason why the ministry was so regularly desperate.

The duplex that came with the property was newer, larger, and more comfortable than The Open Door. Each of the identical halves of the building had a living room, dining room, and kitchen on the ground floor; three bedrooms and a bathroom upstairs; and a full attic and basement. An ample porch spanned the entire front of the house and the main entrances from the sidewalk. Marty Snyder, whose husband was still on the board, was especially enthusiastic about fixing up the new house. She called carpeting retailers, and gave them the opportunity to donate carpeting. She offered others the opportunity to provide padding. The kitchen in the west half of the house, nearest The Open Door, received much needed modernization.

The roofs of both of the buildings leaked and needed to be completely reshingled. Plumbing fixtures and wiring in the new house needed to be replaced, and the exterior badly needed a coat of paint. These projects required professional assistance. Marty solicited bids. Even though funds were available, decisions to proceed were somehow delayed. The leaky toilets remained and the exterior siding was not painted for over a year. The roofs still leaked ten years later. The houses were inhabited by a seemingly immortal breed of cockroaches.

Some of the original board and staff members were beginning to feel burned out. They gave a lot, received little in return, and weren't seeing the dramatic changes either in people or in the buildings that they'd hoped for. The environment was oppressive. Conflicts arose between people whose primary concerns were pragmatic and those whose primary concerns were spiritual. On top of that pressed the inexorable needs of the folks both were attempting to serve.

One factor which delayed refurbishing the new building was widely differing opinions about what to do with it. A survey of the overall picture of human services in the county revealed urgent needs for a shelter for juvenile runaways, residential treatment for drug abusers, residential care for mentally retarded people, and emergency shelter for females eighteen and older. Having both young men and young women sharing sleeping rooms and a single bathroom at The Open Door was becoming an embarrassment in the community.

In May the board of directors approved a proposal to use the building for runaway girls and young women who needed emergency shelter. Bernie and his wife, Mary, were to become licensed as foster parents and live in the west half of the house for the summer. In the fall other houseparents would be recruited. Foster care regulation allowed them to shelter up to four juveniles and several more females who were eighteen or older. The girls would live in the east half of the house, and a door would be cut between the two halves to permit supervision. It wasn't to be just a crash pad. Residence would be limited to girls and women who were willing to engage in counseling and work seriously on solving their problems. There were rules against drugs, alcohol, sex, and violence. Residents would be subjected to a curfew and required to help keep their part of the house neat and clean. The facility was named The Next Door.

Barbie, the same Barbie mentioned earlier, had by then

completed her bachelor's degree in social work. She worked at The Next Door part time and helped Bernie and Mary with everything from supervision and counseling to bookkeeping, cooking and cleaning. Dan and his foster son had moved out of The Open Door into one of the nearby apartments. He was on salary as director of The Open Door, and two other young men were offered free room and board in exchange for staffing The Open Door in the evenings and overnight. Dan and Barbie were planning to be married.

Part of the impetus for making and acting on the proposal for The Next Door was the availability of federal funds for the treatment of drug abuse through the county mental health board. With matching local funds, that body was able to pay for such services as shelter, food, and counseling for drug and alcohol abusers. There was considerable ambivalence to government funding, in part because of the paperwork involved. Not only was keeping statistics and filing reports a distasteful task which took time away from direct service, but the accountability for the use of those funds circumscribed the clientele and services which had to be given priority. The program could no longer be radically flexible and open. The government also frowned on discrimination against non-Christians in hiring practices. For these reasons the ministry decided to forego public funding two years later, and rely on contributions from churches, individuals, and foundations that permitted more freedom. Only saints or fools could be that independent at a time when the organization had no money to pay staff salaries and $1500 in overdue bills.

The summer of 1972 was hectic, and everyone was overworked. Many of the original staff had graduated from college, married, and taken jobs in other parts of the country. It was becoming difficult to find qualified young men who were willing to live for more than a short time at The Open Door, and there were very few applicants for the position of houseparents at The Next Door. Bernie and Mary were eager to move out and join a Christian communal household on the north side of town.

Bernie had his hands full as director of the ministry without running The Next Door and living there as well.

Steve Tamminga, another ordained minister who shared the household with Bernie and Mary, was hired in September to direct the operation of The Next Door. A young couple with two small children moved into The Next Door as houseparents. This staffing configuration, an executive director, two program directors, and two live-in staff persons in each house, remained in place for the next ten years.

The houseparents at The Next Door were Sharon and Nico Seinen. Except for a year-long furlough after their first year, they made The Next Door their home for ten or more years of its existence. After five years of residence, Sharon wrote the following account of their experience:

> One day when Jesus and His disciples were tired and were heading for a solitary place, a crowd of five thousand met them. Jesus had compassion on this crowd because they were like sheep without a shepherd and He taught them. As it grew late, the disciples became concerned that the people had nothing to eat. "You give them something to eat," Jesus said, and the disciples exclaimed over the impossibility of it. Jesus asked them what they had available. There were only five loaves and two fish. But with Jesus, it was enough. Five thousand people were amply fed.
>
> Here at The Doors are the twentieth-century counterparts of the crowd seeking food and Someone to meet deep spiritual and emotional needs.
>
> Five years ago, Nico and I heard Jesus telling us to help feed these kids. Not being as astute as the disciples, we were eager, confident, and idealistic. We moved into The Next Door with three-year-old Pieter, two-month-old Benji, and a dozen high hopes. In only a few days we were crying, like the disciples, "This is impossible! How can we ever meet such overwhelming needs?"
>
> I remember discovering that Janie had head lice and that Debby had scabies after coming upon them cuddling Benji.

I remember Pieter, during his "taste everything stage," finding and bringing a large capsule of some street drug. I remember trying to explain the gospel to a girl who had dabbled in Satanism and was afraid to speak Jesus' name. I remember summer nights with fights outside when we would get so little sleep that just surviving through the next day was all we hoped for.

The tired disciples were told to assess their resources. They had five loaves and two fish. We evaluated our resources and discovered that what we possessed in the areas of money, patience, love, wisdom, and endurance was as inadequate to meet the needs at The Next Door as that little lunch was to feed 5,000.

But through the frightening times, the discouraging times and the just plain tiring times this is what we have learned: THE MEAGERNESS OF WHO WE ARE AND WHAT WE HAVE DOES NOT LIMIT GOD! HE HAS PROVEN FAITHFUL AS OUR SUSTAINER AND THE MULTIPLIER OF OUR RESOURCES.

Many times, just as the freezer was getting empty, a generous donation of meat would arrive. Volunteers have appeared when paid staff badly needed respite. Sometimes when one staff member has lost patience with a particularly abrasive personality, another staff person is able to see potential and give Christ's love.

Staff members who have disagreed vehemently on many issues have been brought to a place of respect and love for each other because of the unity we have in Christ Jesus. And in spite of a witness that is at times a faltering one, people have been pointed to Jesus by the working of the Holy Spirit.

May people continue to be fed, housed, counseled and loved here at The Next Door and The Open Door. As you who support us and we who live and work here realize our own failings and inadequacies, may we rejoice in the confidence that our God is gracious, that His grace is sufficient for us, because His power is made perfect in weakness.

⤳ | *Chapter Three*

Listen to the Lambs

In February of 1975 I began working as a volunteer at The Open Door and The Next Door one or two days a week. For all the organization's problems, for all the disparity between me and most of the rest of the staff, I dearly loved volunteering there.

I most appreciated the opportunity for my work to be an expression of my faith. To provide shelter, food, clothing, and love to anyone there was like offering that service to Christ Himself. The staff regularly discussed the connection between work and faith. This illuminated the meaning and importance of every facet of both. Faith added a completely new dimension to counseling. I had the freedom to say, "You don't deserve to be abused, because God loves you." I was free to delve into emotional problems that had religious beliefs at their base and to approach them theologically as well as psychologically. I could say with some authority, "No, you are not forever damned because you accidentally broke a nun's toe when you were in elementary school. Regardless of what she said, you are forgiven!" When I'd reached the limits of my skill as a counselor and could not help the person more, I could always say, "I'll pray for you." Faith was the net under the tightrope we walked in trying to help people.

I appreciated the personal and emotional involvement of the staff with those they served and my freedom to engage in similar commitment. In some settings this kind of involvement is discouraged. The ministry's encouragement of personal involvement from the beginning gave the work its salty flavor.

I appreciated the variety of experience the ministry permitted me. I saw more different kinds of people and problems than I ever dreamed of in graduate school. The ministry operated on a sociological scrimmage line and encountered a wide range of social, economic, political, psychological, sexual, and criminal problems. It was like a theological laboratory where I could develop ideas and try them out. It was like a spiritual exercise spa where I could work out and come away feeling exhausted but healthier and stronger.

The biggest personal problem I experienced in working at the ministry was the tension between my personal life and the ministry. I didn't want them to be discrete and separate. My family was not intimately involved with the ministry and quickly tired of hearing about it. I could not, of course, leave them to live in the same neighborhood as the ministry. Nor could I forgo my taste for intellectual theology, ritual, and esthetic endeavors, which the ministry could not satisfy. I needed friends whose family situations and interests were similar to mine who also had some sympathy and understanding for my work, and such people were hard to find.

When I became director of The Next Door in August of 1978, the problem intensified. I never got over the feeling of being in a perpetual state of culture shock. Every time I made the eight-mile journey in my car from my suburban home to my office in the poverty ridden neighborhood of Ranney Street, I had to make a shift in feelings, concerns, thought patterns and values. To cite the simplest possible example, cockroaches had completely different meanings at The Next Door and at home. At The Next Door they were an unavoidable fact of life, and I calmly squashed them when they ran across the desk or floor in my office without a second thought. At home, seeing one was a catastrophe! I straddled two different cultures, each an important part of my identity. Wherever I was, I had to make a conscious effort to focus on whichever culture was in the foreground. The other never faded completely into the background and disappeared. I had reasons to laugh and cry in all the wrong places. If maturity is the ability to live gracefully with ambiguity, I achieved it only to a moderate degree.

In middle-class terms, being director of The Next Door meant that I was at least theoretically responsible for everything that went on there. On site I was more likely to be described as "the crazy broad who runs the place." Neither was accurate. I kept The Next Door open and tried to make it livable for houseparents and guests. I tried to help people and to show God's love. However, I rarely felt that I was fully responsible or truly in charge of anything that happened at The Next Door. My main function was to cope.

A major task was to make sure that staff was available around the clock. Fortunately, the Seinens were houseparents throughout my tenure as director. Besides being deeply committed to the ministry, they were flexible about scheduling and supremely reliable. Sharon and Nico and I were the only ones paid to be there, and funding was so sparse that our paychecks arrived late half the time. Hiring additional staff to give each of us two days a week off was out of the question. I had to rely on volunteers working shifts lasting three or four hours. Some came once a week; others more often; still others worked less frequently.

The Jesus People were no longer in evidence as a group and the youth ministry staff was no longer a tightly-knit group that shared and did everything together. Fewer young people were willing to commit their lives devotedly to a ministry such as this. Within certain parameters I was willing to give anyone a chance to volunteer. Since the organization was a ministry, it was logical that the people who worked there should all be Christians. I was unwilling to judge a prospective volunteer's theology from my liberal Presbyterian point of view and unable to be responsible for the morality of their lives in general. Therefore, the main criterion for Christianity was active involvement in an established Christian church or fellowship. I hoped that they would be guided by their own traditions in matters of ethical conduct, in the examples they set, and in the ways they treated people. I hoped that faith was the primary motivating factor in working at The Next Door. I hoped that our evangelistic efforts would be supported, or at least not undermined.

Except for occasional maintenance projects, I used only women. This avoided the seductive games troubled female residents were inclined to play with male staff. I required that volunteers were over the age of eighteen because I didn't want to be responsible for younger people getting into trouble. I avoided using young women who had used our services within the past six months or those who seemed likely to find themselves in need of shelter in the near future. To work alone at The Next Door and cope with whatever happened was a formidable responsibility requiring good judgment, loving acceptance of people despite their appearance and behavior, and a firm but gentle exercise of authority. I needed people who were mature enough to learn those skills quickly.

I tried several recruiting strategies. Stories about volunteers, and urgent pleas for new ones, appeared in our newsletter periodically. Speaking engagements sometimes resulted in new volunteers. I telephoned pastors of supportive churches and asked for names of members of their congregations who could be approached. Current volunteers and board members recruited from among their friends and acquaintances. Local colleges and universities sent us students for practical training in social work.

The result was a corps of women of various ages whose backgrounds spanned the range of tradition in the local Christian community. We had Pentecostal women, Baptists, and charismatics; Reformed, Christian Reformed, and Presbyterian women; Congregationalists, Methodists, and occasionally an Episcopalian or a Catholic. Some had master's degrees; some hadn't finished high school. A few were college students. Others were divorced women with young children. Some were single professional women. Several were women with adult children, who arrived with a wealth of common sense and compassion. Some were retired from careers or had handicaps of their own. Nearly all were extremely reliable and dedicated.

Keeping good volunteers was just as important as recruitment. Because I had loved my volunteer work so much, and because the availability of The Next Door depended upon volunteers, I tried to treat them very well. I wanted them to have the same freedom I'd had to relate to individuals in their own ways. I wanted them to experience the same satisfaction I'd felt in doing a ministry that had real meaning. I wanted to help them learn about the unfortunate people in our society, and to help them develop skills to do the kinds of ministries to which they felt personally called.

My training program consisted mainly of my telling the prospective volunteer what she needed to know. I used a checklist. I gave her a tour of the buildings and introduced her to people. I asked her to attend a drop-in to talk casually with the visitors and get a feel for the work. I explained the organizational structure, the general intention of the ministry, and my view of what was happening and how things ought to be done. She needed to be able to answer inquiries of various types from the community, inquiries from those who might use our services, from the network of other agencies and students checking out referral resources, and from prospective supporters. I counted on volunteers to be spokespersons for the ministry, enlisting support from their own churches and acquaintances. A volunteer needed to be oriented to routine procedures such as inducting a new guest and locking up the office and the house at night. I taught her techniques for getting people to do what she wanted them to do, and for careful listening. In the beginning she could work with me or with another volunteer until she felt comfortable being at The Next Door alone, or until I needed her desperately, which usually came first.

As we progressed through my checklist, she would ask

questions and express her anxieties. It was no good telling her that she would never see anything bad happen or that she was actually safe from violence, theft, and vandalism. I told her how to take reasonable precautions and where to call for help. There weren't more than two or three violent episodes a year at The Next Door while I was director. None involved volunteers having to receive medical treatment. No one ever got raped there, thank God! Still, danger was always imminent enough that we were aware that we were laying down our lives. I was always surprised that so many people were willing to do that. If she qualified by her willingness, like the early staff, I took her to lunch and we became friends. Volunteers were a great source of emotional support to me. They understood the cultural and spiritual tensions in my life. When I needed to talk over problems and ventilate frustration, they were always ready to listen and understand. I tried never to let them forget how important they were to the ministry and how much I appreciated them.

Most agencies that provide residential care employ at least one paid staff person per client for round-the-clock supervision, and for clerical and janitorial support. Only in recent years could the ministry afford a part-time secretary. Until then The Open Door maintained a year-round average of six crashers a night with only three paid staff. The Next Door sheltered an average of three or four young women with the same number of staff, a more manageable ratio. The maximum capacity of The Next Door was seven or eight people. Visits from neighbors, male and female, or from former residents usually doubled the number of people we saw in a day. They came in and asked to use the phone; requested bandaids, aspirin, tampons, or food; or just said, "I've got to talk to somebody right away!" The latter might have meant anything from threats of violence or suicide to an urgent need for mending a pair of jeans. Sometimes the staff would have long, quiet afternoons when we could read, do housework, or knit and have leisurely conversations with the guests. When nothing was happening, we served the purpose of offering consistently sustained availability. Within five minutes we could be as busy as a one-armed paperhanger with the itch!

People came to The Doors through a variety of channels. Some people heard of us on a street corner or in a park when they asked where they might sleep for the night. Some telephoned the twenty-four-hour crisis line which served as a clearing house for mental health services, substance abuse treatment, and many other kinds of assistance the community provided. Most human service agencies in town were aware of the youth ministry and referred people needing shelter to it. The route of access was the front door. Those who arrived there had little or no money and had a wide variety of problems which precipitated crisis needs for shelter. I classified these problems into five inter-related clusters: physical abuse, mental illness, drug and alcohol abuse, legal problems, and physical or developmental disabilities.

People always asked me if I sheltered battered wives. Another agency in town had the space and the secure location to accommodate them and their children. Most of the battered women who came to me hadn't married the men who beat them up. I came to think of any kind of domestic abuse in one large, hideous category. Nine times out of ten, a woman who is abused by a sexual partner was abused as a child. A woman who was abused as a child will frequently abuse her own children or permit them to be abused. One would think that it would be a good idea to remove these kids from their homes and put them in good foster homes. But the people we saw who had spent years in foster care seemed to have fewer of the skills and strengths to take care of themselves as adults than the ones who had endured years of abuse. After about two years I became aware, to my horror, that easily half and probably three quarters of the women who came to me had been sexually abused in childhood. The perpetrators were rarely strangers. The shame and denial that accompanied this situation were every bit as damaging as the acts themselves.

Mental health problems precipitated a sizeable portion of the crises which resulted in the need for shelter. During the seventies we saw a trend toward treating victims of mental illness in the community rather than in institutions. Outpatient treatment is less costly for the state, and it is better for the patient to have more personal freedom. Some, however, were prone to interpersonal or financial crises which resulted in their leaving or being evicted from wherever they had been living. My degree in counseling had not prepared me to do therapy for severely disordered persons. But my being calm and accepting seemed to make people feel better. I also developed a routine of keeping psychotropic medication locked in my office and insisting that it be taken consistently as prescribed. Without medication people were more likely to become too disturbed and disruptive to stay at The Next Door. When that happened I had to try to get the individual admitted to a hospital, a complicated and time-consuming procedure. When I could not convince the mental health people that the person was dangerous to herself or to others, I had little choice except to send her back out on the street.

Another cluster of problems involved the judicial system. I hated going to court. Twice I was a witness in custody hearings involving abuse. After being supportive and sympathetic for years, I had to give testimony that would not help my friend to get her child back. Both instances were incredibly painful for everyone concerned. A few times I went to court just to be supportive to people who were guilty of any of a variety of crimes: selling magazines door to door without a license, refusing to clean up garbage, shoplifting, malicious destruction of property, or some degree of assault. Trials always occurred six to eight months after an arrest. By that time any remorse a person might have felt was dissipated, and the most just decision felt like personal persecution. I didn't have the credentials to be an expert advocate, and felt as helpless as the defendant in the inexorable process.

About one in five people who came to The Next Door had a physical disability such as mild retardation, diabetes, epilepsy or cerebral palsy. I remember one young woman who had cerebral palsy, who had one of the most winning smiles I'd ever seen in my life. She was just as cute as a button! The first time I met her, I said, "You know, when I was about sixteen I remember seeing a poster in the grocery store, a picture of a little girl with cerebral palsy. She was just adorable, and she looked just like you."

The young woman smiled again, and said, "Let me show you something." She dragged herself upstairs with her crutches, and returned with a fistful of yellowed newspaper clippings. She had been a national poster child for cerebral palsy in the late fifties.

Many of the people who came to us were physically ill. Colds and flu were the most common ailments, but we saw everything from genital herpes to cancer, from false pregnancies to broken bones. Whenever we could, we encouraged our guests to use the hospital outpatient clinics, but this usually entailed a two- to three-week wait for an appointment. Some of our guests had Medicaid, and could make appointments with private physicians who would take Medicaid patients. The number of doctors who would take them decreased with the diminishing benefits and increasing paperwork. From time to time there were physicians and dentists on our board of directors who would examine people, give us advice, and write prescriptions. They enlisted the help of colleagues who gave us prompt appointments in their offices, and did not charge for their services. If we didn't screen complaints carefully and use all other resources, we found ourselves in doctors' offices three and four times a week. This was too much for a physician with a busy practice.

People who were unaccustomed to good care as children often panicked at the slightest discomfort. They would believe themselves to be seriously ill, regardless of any doctor's assurances. Sometimes they lied outright about their conditions. Unless the guest was willing to let me be present during an examination or consultation, I could not verify information about her condition. Even if I had been responsible for obtaining medical services, her confidentiality was protected by law.

Usually I treated the individual as if she were telling me the truth, and would perhaps hear a different story when she tired of the regimen of treatment. Some people denied the serious-ness of their illnesses and stopped cooperating with treatment long before it should have been withdrawn.

When the houseparents and I could not persuade our resi-dents to wait for appointments with private physicians or clinics, or to trust the doctors we took them to see, we were pressured to take them to the emergency room. They seemed to love going there. We had to balance our feelings about waiting in the hospital for several hours, often knowing that we were misusing the hospital's services, with the fear of allowing a serious condi-tion to go untreated.

Once we had a small, handicapped, depressed, and very pas-sive guest who slipped on the ice and injured her ankle. She was so hypersensitive about the pain that she flinched and cried out when my hands were six inches in the air above the injury. The accident happened on a weekend, and Sharon Seinen treated her as she would have treated her own children. She kept the leg elevated, administered ice packs, and would not let the guest put any weight on the foot. The leg and foot could be moved, albeit with some discomfort, and it looked for all the world like it was moderately sprained. All parties agreed that we would make an appointment to have it x-rayed if it didn't feel better after the weekend.

Then the guest's boyfriend arrived on the scene. He was someone we knew and loved, a goodhearted young man, but he had a habit of losing his temper and behaving erratically. His diagnosis was that her leg was broken, and he demanded that she be taken to the trauma and emergency center immediately. We had already been there twice within the past week with folks with hypochondriac symptoms. Besides that, the lady was not eligible for Medicaid. It would have taken her two years to pay for the services, if she didn't default altogether. I reiterated my promise to make an appointment for x-rays, which would cost much less than the emergency room. He would not hear of any delay, and was insulted that cost should be a factor in selecting treatment. I finally said to the injured woman, "You are an adult and a free agent. If you want to go to the emergency room, it's up to you. But I'm not going to take you there."

She wanted to go, and the boyfriend found her a ride. When they returned several hours later, they informed us that a bone in the ankle was indeed cracked. The doctor didn't put a cast on it right away—in fact, the treatment he prescribed was exactly what we were already doing. Still, I was profoundly embarrassed. My only recourse was to swallow my pride and tell the couple that I was very sorry. I promised that we would let her stay at The Next Door and take care of her until the bone healed. I even thanked the young man for taking care of the situation for us!

One evening later that week I watched a special program on educational television about Mother Teresa of Calcutta. When it was over, I turned off the set and began to cry. Mother Teresa picked people up off the pavement and gave them clean straw mats to sleep on, some rice, and lots of tender loving care. She sheltered thousands of people. I only had four or five at a time. Never mind that we had to provide heat for the building, regular beds to sleep on, outrageously expensive medical treatment, a high protein diet, a certain amount of junk food, and a television set that worked! Mother Teresa would not refuse to take someone to the hospital with a broken leg!

Marlin was sitting in his reclining chair, smoking his pipe and listening to me ventilate my feelings. When I finished, he calmly took his pipe out of his mouth and said, "You know what I think?"

"No," I said. "For Heaven's sake, tell me what you think!"

"I think," he continued, the corners of his mouth beginning to twitch, "that you just shot the Nobel Peace Prize all to hell!"

I never again tried to compare myself to Mother Teresa.

We were not a treatment facility like a hospital or a clinic. Except with minors, who were essentially foster children and governed by foster home regulations, we had no more

responsibility for our guests than a private individual who invited someone to spend the night. We did not call the folks who
came to us clients. The typical guest suffered from some combination of physical abuse, mental illness, legal difficulties and
physical problems. We had no professional credentials to do
very much to help any of them. By and large they were not
asking for professional help, and did not want to be called
clients. They wanted to be loved and cared for. As I came to see
their suffering and to understand their struggles, I learned to
love them. Sometimes I thought it would break my heart.

I remember sitting in church one Sunday morning early in
my ministry. I had had a difficult week, and was tired and
discouraged. The choir sang the familiar anthem, "Listen to the
Lambs." "Listen to the lambs," they sang, "all a-crying; all
a-crying; all, all a-crying." I could hear all the complaints from
all the people I had encountered throughout the week bleating
deafeningly in my head. Lambs are such noisy creatures, so
easily terrified and so difficult to comfort. And there are so
blessed many of them!

Then in the anthem came the comforting words from Isaiah
40, "He shall feed his flock like a shepherd, and carry the young
lambs in his bosom. . . ." I knew then that it was His flock, not
mine. The lambs were His to care for in a way that I could not.
I sang that song to myself after that, hundreds of times while
driving to and from work. "Lambs" became the term I used in
my prayers for the people who came to me. A lamb is what our
Savior Himself was called. "Lamb" is a good term for anyone
who is in need of shepherding. I needed it as desperately as
those who came to me. I felt myself being led and carried.

Designing ongoing programs for multiple-problem "lambs"
was about as frustrating as trying to keep paint on The Open
Door. The Open Door staff generally had a lot more youth and
vigor than I had. They intermittently provided a range of activities for both men and women from beach parties to Bible study.
Outings permitted bonding between those who came for drop-
in and staff. Having lively, healthy fun together was a good idea,

but even a beach party required huge amounts of planning and stamina. Everything that could possibly go wrong usually did. The participants would smoke dope on the bus, make babies in the dunes, start fights among themselves, get sunburns, mosquito bites, and poison ivy, and complain about everything. I felt that if I had to spend my time coping with complaints and problems, I could do so more effectively in my office, one at a time. While there were few planned activities at The Next Door, the facility was available to both male and female nonresidents for counseling and other needs that arose. Sharon undertook emotional support and teaching of skills to new mothers who came to her. I read aloud a book on black history, a chapter at a time, to a couple who needed to develop pride in their race.

Those who frequented the Doors were no longer willing to attend Bible study because they had nothing better to do. Their reliability for making and keeping commitments was extremely low. If five or ten people indicated an interest in such a program, one or two might actually show up—sometimes. They stayed away in droves when it rained or snowed, when the weather was too nice to stay indoors, or when something else came up. Bible study worked better when conducted one-to-one in the individual's apartment or when conducted at regular times during drop-in with whoever happened to be present and willing to participate. Informal worship services were a continuing feature of the drop-in program at The Open Door, and a majority of people who came for drop-in attended worship when it was offered.

Programming at The Next Door was more individual and casual. In the beginning I had an intense distaste for even implied pressure on residents and others to subject themselves to indoctrination. It took me three years to develop a systematic plan for evangelism with which I felt sufficiently comfortable both theologically and humanly to advocate it and teach it to other staff. This is described in another chapter. In the meantime we simply answered questions as they arose and talked about our faith when we felt like it and it seemed appropriate. Behavioral changes that were made, though we prayed and worked heartily for them, were essentially between the individuals and the Holy Spirit. Before the guests would believe us when we told them the Good News, we had to be Good News.

There was no way we could assess, let alone serve, all of the physical, emotional and spiritual needs of everyone who came to us. "Radical flexibility" was a term used to describe the early ministry at The Open Door. It was the term I used to describe our offering ourselves as Christians, as counselors, and as human beings to those who came to us, and relating to each one as she presented herself to us moment by moment. One girl needed to be taught to shampoo her hair properly, another had to be taught not to cook hot dogs on the burner of our electric stove. When one was willing to talk, we listened. When she was ready to listen, we talked. If she needed food or clothing, we gave it to her. When she was in the mental hospital or in prison, we visited her. When she was ready to do something constructive, such as go back to school or look for a job, we gave her all the support and reinforcement we were able to give. We began with whatever she was experiencing at the moment, let her lead us, and exerted gentle influence whenever we could. When she was ready to do something destructive, like attempt suicide or prostitute herself or commit a crime, we did our best to talk her out of it. Failing that we tried to persuade her to do it later, and preferably somewhere else!

I think I would have gone out of my mind if I had been required to follow conventional concepts of programming. It would have been impossible to have evaluated our services according to the number of people who learned to live normal, productive lives. Instead we strove to treat people fairly, lovingly, and mercifully, regardless of what they did.

To illustrate how this worked, and what we were up against, I'll introduce a typical guest, a hypothetical composite I'll call Debbie. Debbie's parents were divorced when she was four years old. She was left with her mother, who was an alcoholic. Her mother had a series of boyfriends who lived in the household from time to time. One of them liked Debbie even better than her mother, and fondled her and played with her in a way she'd never experienced before. Debbie was willing to do any-thing he asked, and he asked a lot. Then he went away. There were other temporary stepfathers, some more drunk and abu-sive than others. Debbie had problems when she went to school. She couldn't concentrate. She thought she was the only little girl in the world who knew what she knew, and did what she did. The mother couldn't cope with the school problems. By this time Debbie's father had remarried, and Debbie went to live with him. The stepmother was young and impatient. Debbie did ornery, destructive things to get attention from her father. She'd also learned to be very seductive. Eventually her father was forced to choose between his wife and his daughter, and Debbie was placed in foster care. Foster homes aren't all bad, but they're not home. If she ran away often enough, the social worker would have to give her back to one of her parents.

By the time she was a teenager, Debbie had learned to walk like a victim, talk like a victim, and act in ways that made her a victim. Inevitably she met her Prince Charming, who, of course, was looking for a victim. He was older than she, and taught her to drink and smoke marijuana to feel good. He required her to accommodate other men for money, and he beat her up.

All Debbie had ever wanted in her whole life was to be taken care of. All of her misguided energy had been directed toward that end. None had been directed toward learning to take care of herself and to make independent decisions. She had never learned to take pleasure in doing new things, nor satisfaction from her own accomplishments. She was willing to do anything for the men in her life, no matter how humiliating, and it all ended in failure. Neither of her parents would take her back. The Department of Social Services could not put her in another foster home. She was seventeen and had been uncooperative in the past, and there were not enough foster homes to go around. Anyway, she didn't want a foster home. She didn't know what she wanted. The loss of Prince Charming, never mind what I thought of him, coupled with rejection from her parents, was a trauma roughly equivalent to two deaths in her immediate family. But she felt too guilty to mourn.

Of course I had no way of knowing all this when Debbie walked into my office for the first time. I only saw before me a young woman with long hair, wearing jeans and a t-shirt. Her eyes darted furtively around the room. Her shoulders were hunched as if she were afraid I would hit her. She sat down without looking at me and propped up her head with her hand, her elbow on her skinny stomach. Her posture told me that she would be profoundly passive.

My first task was to make her feel comfortable and welcome. As soon as I had determined her age, I assured her that she indeed could stay. I asked her to fill out a "green sheet" that gave me information about her health, her religious preference, and whom we should contact in case of emergency. I explained that The Next Door was able to provide shelter, food, personal items such as combs and toothbrushes, counseling, referrals for medical care or schooling, and assistance in looking for a job. I also went over our simple sheet of rules with her. We wanted her to be out of bed by nine in the morning, to help keep The Next Door clean, to eat supper with the houseparents five evenings a week, and to be in by ten o'clock during the week and midnight on weekends. She was allowed to use the laundry on certain days of the week and to use the phone with permission for local calls. Drugs, alcohol, sexual intercourse, weapons, and pets were not permitted. She was invited to stay for two weeks at the outset, and could request an extension at the end of that time if we were getting along well.

The Seinens and I did everything we could to get along well with her. I asked if she had any questions. She had none. I encouraged her to ask questions later. Then I showed her around, introduced her to the houseparents and the other residents, and helped her carry her bags, if she had any, upstairs to a bedroom. If she was hungry, I helped her get something to eat in the kitchen. If she wasn't hungry, I offered her a cup of coffee or Kool-Aid, and asked how she came to be in need of a place to stay.

I always heard the story backwards, the boyfriend first, then the foster parents, and much later about her parents and her childhood. I asked about school. Finishing high school would have taken several years, and she had no interest in school. She guessed she would have to get a job. I was the last person in the world to discourage her from trying to get a job, but I had a pretty good idea she wouldn't succeed. Still, I tried to help.

It took her three hours to read the want ads. I saved her time by asking what kind of work she might be able to do, skimming the ads for her, and circling the ones for which she might be qualified. I knew which restaurants hired girls to be waitresses and expected them to be prostitutes. I could also spot any two ads in the same neighborhood, so she did not have to trek from one end of town to the other and back. I asked her to fill out a mock job application for me. She would not be called for an interview if she didn't know the address and phone number of the place where she was staying. The chances of being called for an interview would increase by about twenty-five percent if she filled in all the blanks and spelled everything correctly. References were a big problem. She could not think of any responsible adult she had known for over a year.

She procrastinated going out and trying. I didn't push her very hard. I arranged for a haircut with the local beauty school. I coached her about which clothes to wear, and gave her something other than jeans and a t-shirt if I had it. She didn't know how to find her way to an address in a strange part of the city. I couldn't drive her there in my car because there was no one to fill in for me in the office, and she had to learn to find her own way around sooner or later. She hated riding a bus, and was scared to death of it. I knew the routes and the time schedules, and sent her with another resident who knew which one she should get on. She couldn't read fast enough to see the street signs, and didn't know where to look for the numbers on the buildings. I drew the best map I possibly could. If she ever found where she was supposed to go, she would have to talk to a stranger who might not be friendly. He would be in the position of judging her suitability for a job, and she couldn't look him in the eye. If she were hired, she would have had one of the most difficult and demanding jobs this society has to offer, most likely cooking fast foods or cleaning motel rooms. She would be afraid to ask questions, afraid to let anyone know that she didn't know how to do what she was hired to do. She would become scared and defensive when her work was criticized, and her supervisor would fire her because he thought she was lazy.

The overwhelming probability was that she would get on the wrong bus in spite of my efforts, ride around for a couple of hours, and give up. By then she may have decided to go back to Prince Charming or may have met a new one. She was almost certain to come back to The Next Door in a few months. By then she would probably have made herself known to the mental health network by attempting suicide, or she'd have become pregnant.

It all seemed like an exercise in futility. I scolded myself a lot in four years for not having done more for her, for not having pushed her harder. On the other hand, it was prideful to expect that I could overcome years of victimization in two weeks. I had learned to know her and she had learned to know me. In caring for her and listening to her, I caught little glimpses of her potential and little pieces of evidence that God had been working in her life all along. She did not come to us by chance, but because God had a purpose in mind. He wanted her to be free, to be part of His household and His kingdom. Whatever good came of her stay in The Next Door, whatever love she experienced, whatever she learned, was part of His plan, the whole of which we could not see. Nothing we did lovingly for the least member of His kingdom, no matter how trivial, was truly wasted.

≈ | *Chapter Four*

Love and Conviviality

When someone came to The Next Door asking for shelter, she was essentially asking for the gift of life itself. Needing shelter is a crisis of emotional and social survival. Though a woman was not likely to die if she were turned away from The Next Door, she might have found herself at risk of physical abuse, rape, and the loss of her personal possessions. Being without a place to live made her feel as if there were no place on the planet where she belonged. If she had been forced to leave her former home, she experienced this as rejection at an intimate, personal level. These feelings could drive her more deeply into despair, mental illness, or drug abuse. A crisis, however, is also an opportunity. The offer of shelter was a concrete witness to an individual's right to exist. Hospitality was an affirmation of a person's value as a human being. The power to offer shelter amounted to power over a profoundly important contingency in a person's life.

It was the responsibility of the Seinens and me to use that power lovingly and to administer it with mercy and grace. Our program goal was to offer shelter to as many people as possible and to make that shelter the best we could offer. We considered ourselves successful when our guests moved on to more stable and appropriate living situations, and when their departures were less urgent and traumatic than their arrivals. Our greatest joy was to say to a frightened, desperate person, "You are welcome. We are glad to have you here." Our greatest pain was to say, "We are sorry, we can't let you stay here."

Three main factors limited our ability to offer shelter and to provide it as long as it was needed. The most obvious of these factors was the limitation of our physical space. We had only eight beds and could not install more without serious over-crowding. An equally important factor was the limitation of our time and energy to attend to residents' needs and to make their visits pleasant and productive. A third limiting factor was con-cern for the quality of the environment.

Much as we disliked the idea of judging people, if we were to be responsible for the quality of the environment, we had to make decisions about behavior that was or was not permitted there. I use the old-fashioned word *authority* to denote this ordi-nary function of making judgments about the acceptability and preferability of behavior. To decide for a group what behaviors are allowed and disallowed is to exercise authority. To shrink from making those decisions was to decide in favor of chaos. Not to use the power available to us to put those decisions into effect was irresponsible. One might think this is a matter of simple common sense. Where there was diversity of opinions and expectations as extensive as that among the ministry staff and between the staff and the guests, common sense could not be assumed; nor was it simple. By articulating our concerns honestly we came to understand each other and develop a truly common sense about the situation so that we were unified in our exercise of authority.

One of our concerns was safety. Another was respect for basic standards of decency in the community. Our constituents, those who supported the ministry, expected us to provide a whole-some environment, a place where people were not exposed to violence, theft, illicit sexual activity, alcohol, and drugs. It was understood that we did not have absolute control over residents' behavior and that these things happened occasionally. We were obliged, however, not to permit such activities to continue unchecked when they came to our attention.

Along with these concerns for the safety of guests and the opinion of the community, we had to assume responsibility for our own health and well-being. There were limits to the amount of stress we on the staff could endure for long periods of time. We needed to maintain a quality of life at The Next Door which permitted a degree of comfort and tranquillity, and mitigated avoidable frustrations. The frustrations that most quickly wore out our friendly dispositions involved our own needs for comfort, privacy, and rest. All of these were regularly and willingly sacrificed because of the poverty of the environment and unavoidable demands of troubled people. Dirt, clutter, noise, unwashed dishes, and hostile attitudes on the part of guests were standard fare which we countered with patience and good humor. We accepted the fact that people came to us in a state of crisis, and that their abilities to control themselves were already stretched thin. We had no desire to make impossible demands of people who were barely able to cope with another day of living. We accepted the fact that our guests had habits, lifestyles, and housekeeping standards that were different from ours. Our intent was not to impose our preferences upon them as if they were serious moral issues. We did not adopt an attitude of superiority, or expect special courtesy and subservience because of our role as authority figures. We tried, as far as possible, to accommodate their feelings, their needs, and their individuality, and to make them feel comfortable and accepted. We were, however, human, and our tolerance was limited. Long periods of constant unpleasantness, hostility, noise, disorder, and frequent interruptions of any activity we attempted made us angry, resentful, and irritable. When we perceived our discomfort as unnecessary and counterproductive, we found it very difficult to serve people cheerfully and tenderly.

Over time, the necessity for a minimal level of the quality of life that permitted us to offer safe and decent shelter became apparent. A convenient and happy word for this quality of life is *conviviality,* adapted from the Latin roots meaning to live or enjoy life together. Conviviality, as I use the term, is a basic level of safety, decency, comfort and well-being that permits people to live together. It includes such things as sufficient food, warmth, bodily protection and rest; respect for privacy, autonomy, and personal possessions; mutual understandings about the use of shared space and facilities; and respect for each person's physical comfort, tastes, and values. The level of convivial comfort is variable according to the needs and tolerance levels of the people involved at any given time, the duration of discomfort, and the kinds of changes that are possible. It depends, too, on the frequency and kinds of annoyances individuals are able to put up with and their capacities for repeated forgiveness. It was far better for us to be honest about our feelings and our limitations and to make changes wherever they were possible than to make artificial sacrifices and harbor resentment that could explode later. Conviviality was a survival issue. Without it we could not sustain our dispositions at The Next Door day after day and do the kind of ministry we were there for. Without it guests could not stand to live there either, nor could they progress toward solving their problems.

The hospitality that the Seinens and I would like to have offered openly and unconditionally had to be tempered by the limitations of space and personnel to support conviviality. These limitations forced us into a situation of triage, which I would have preferred to avoid. Triage is a term that is used in medical emergencies to denote the decision process that is used when more patients are brought into a hospital than can be immediately treated. Someone has to sort among patients who will likely survive a delay in treatment, those who will probably not survive even with immediate and intensive treatment, and those for whom immediate treatment will make the difference between life and death or between full recovery and permanent disability. As terrible as it is to have to make such decisions, someone must assume responsibility for them. Decisions about who received priority for space and attention at The Next Door were not imminently life threatening, but they were decisions of serious consequence. The factors on which those decisions were made were always relative and based on highly subjective hunches.

Generally we took people on a first-come, first-served basis, and accepted any woman who requested shelter if she were within our age limits and a bed was available. We did not refuse people because their need, in our opinion, was insufficient. If a woman had left her previous residence peremptorily and without having made other plans, she probably had important reasons for doing so. Even if she had an income, she needed time to find an apartment and to assemble the funds for the security deposit on it. Such a woman was just as much at the mercy of street life as one who was forced out of her home by eviction or violence and had no resources at all. I discouraged people from coming to The Next Door who had other places where they could live safely or who were eligible for other programs in the community. The Next Door was to be a shelter of last resort, and we preferred to keep a bed available for those who might otherwise have to spend the night without a roof over their heads or to subject themselves to the degradations of street life. Clearly the availability of a bed at any given time depended upon myriad decisions about intakes and how long we allowed people to stay. In that sense, triage occurred even though we were not sorting urgent cases on the front porch.

A more subtle form of triage occurred when The Next Door was full. Seven or eight very troubled young women overcrowded the available living space and overextended the energy of the staff. Guests became irritable because there was insufficient privacy and the house was constantly noisy. There were long waits for use of the bathroom, the laundry and the telephone. Personal belongings were misplaced or stolen. Arguments and fights occured, and drug use became difficult to control. As conviviality deteriorated, some residents became depressed and passive. Others slyly avoided encounters with the staff, and used

The Next Door to provide physical amenities while they engaged in a wide variety of destructive and disruptive behavior. As a result, the most capable residents wearied of the turmoil and left The Next Door in favor of the kinds of living situations we hoped to enable them to avoid. The least capable people became totally unmanageable, sometimes psychotic or violent, and had to leave at our behest. Both extremes constituted failure for us. Triage occurred with or without our deliberate participation, whether we wanted to assume responsibility for it or not.

In the simplest possible terms, we had three options for assuming responsibility for triage: We could control the number of people we accepted at any given time, we could restrict the kinds of people we were willing to serve, and we could limit the length of time we allowed people to stay. The first option was by far the simplest. We could have declared our capacity to be any number we chose, and that number could even be variable. The number of people we could serve with conviviality depended upon the frequency and intensity of attention each one required, and how well they were able to get along with each other and the staff. When the household was running smoothly, however, we were always tempted to make room for one more, and we were always hesitant to refuse someone who knocked on the door in the middle of the night.

Restricting the kinds of people we accepted was a more complex issue. Some shelters restrict the target population by specializing in one cluster of problems. Shelters that serve battered women, women with problem pregnancies, people with mental problems, or abusers of drugs or alcohol are examples. The Next Door did not specialize because we did not see ourselves as a treatment center, and because Kalamazoo had a wide variety of specialized treatment facilities. Specialization permitted people with several serious problems, or with unidentified problems, to fall through the cracks. People who are both mentally ill and mentally retarded, for instance, were often deemed inappropriate for treatment by facilities specializing in either of those problems. An alternative to specialization was to restrict our acceptance of people with certain kinds of problems. We might have excluded people, for instance, who had criminal records, or who had been patients in the state mental hospital, or who had a high propensity for violence. This was generally impractical because people simply refrained from giving us this information if they thought they would be rejected if we knew. Part of our witness was to offer shelter regardless of a person's past history. Sometimes we were able to live convivially with people who had proven too difficult for other programs to handle precisely because we did not ask for case histories and started completely afresh. We found it unwise, however, to accept as residents those who were too dysfunctional, due to drug use, mental illness, or mental retardation, to talk with us. Residents had to be able to give us information about themselves, their health, and their problems, and to understand our minimal expectations of them while they were living at The Next Door.

Occasionally we refused people who had abused or misused The Next Door in the recent past. Nico proposed the motto, "We'll try anything twice," which became a rule of thumb with difficult people. That permitted everyone a second chance. We were willing to give third and fourth and fifth chances if we were given any reason to hope those chances would be successful, or if sufficient time had elapsed. A flexible, practical guideline for the length of time we restricted return visits was the accumulated length of our contact with a person. If she initially stayed for ten days and we had to ask her to leave, we were willing to give her another chance after ten days. If after another ten-day stay she was uncooperative, she could not return for at least thirty days, and then only if she were able to show some evidence of growth or change in the interim.

When I became its director, The Next Door was licensed as a private foster care home and we could take girls as young as fourteen. After a violent incident which I will describe in a subsequent chapter, the state required a group home license for which The Next Door was ineligible. From that time forward, seventeen years of age became our lower age limit. The upper age limit was arbitrarily set at twenty-five. The reason for this was that in the early days of community treatment of mental illness, The Next Door found itself hosting women in their middle years who had spent much of their lives in institutions. Some were unable to keep themselves clean and groomed and to make their own breakfasts and lunches. They needed more intensive supervision and longer term care than The Next Door was able to provide. It was an injustice to them and to the community to pretend that we could help them. In time, the mental health system developed other resources for these women. I made exceptions to the upper age limit, if other agencies or individuals, particularly people from churches, were willing to provide services like transportation and ongoing emotional sup-port for their referrals.

Controlling the duration of residence was the third way we could maintain our census at a convivial level and assure the availability of a bed at any given time. During my years as a volunteer, The Next Door limited residence to two weeks. At that time there were other residential programs in the commu-nity for both juveniles and adults with specific problems which offered longer term care. When the emphasis in community mental health shifted to shorter term treatment, The Next Door undertook longer term shelter. There were some disadvantages to this policy. Some people lost their motivation to do anything for themselves in the absence of urgency to find another place to stay. Referral agencies sometimes took their own sweet time in arranging subsequent placements for their clients. We found ourselves spending more time with more deeply troubled peo-ple, some of whom deteriorated before our eyes. Nevertheless, longer term care was my distinct preference. I didn't like having to rush people into decisions about where to go next. I enjoyed having the leisure to get to know them better, to explore their options, and to allow those options to materialize before hus-tling them out. I also liked to see real changes in people. It seemed that the opportunity to see a turn for the better despite temporary setbacks generally improved when I wasn't working against time.

My postgraduate education in exercising authority and maintaining conviviality at The Next Door was the gift of a young woman I'll call Jackie, who was living there at the time I became the director. She was intelligent, energetic, gutsy, and had no family at all. The Seinens and I desperately wanted to see her through the tail-end of her adolescence and launch her lovingly into the independence for which she was so well suited. But Jackie had a serious problem with following rules. I had a theory that she was breaking rules in order to test how much we loved her, and that once she felt secure she would learn to cooperate. It seemed to me that the times when she behaved most unacceptably were the times when she most needed love, forgiveness and the assurance of a home. I also had the naive notion that we were able to put up with virtually anything. When behavior such as staying out late at night, drug use, and fighting absolutely required some kind of action on my part, I assigned extra household chores, imposed early curfews, and finally resorted to asking her to leave for one or more nights at a time.

After about six weeks of that nonsense, Jackie decided she wasn't going to be put out of her home any more. When I told her to leave, she simply planted herself in the living room and said, "I'm not going anywhere. I live here and I have a right to stay." I felt I had no choice but to call the police. The pattern had been established that when someone was asked to leave in the presence of an officer and refused to do so, she would be charged with trespassing. When the police arrived, Jackie told them that The Next Door was her home and that she had no intention of leaving. They asked questions about how long she had lived there, whether she had her own room and her own bed, and where her belongings were stored. Finally they agreed that The Next Door was indeed her legal residence, and that she could not be arrested for trespassing if she refused to leave. If we wanted her to leave, we would have to go through a civil eviction procedure. That would take about a month.

I was immediately aware that if I could not make anyone leave The Next Door I had no control whatever over anything that might go on there. Much as I hated to do it, I explained privately to the police that I had found marijuana in her room. Another resident told me it was there, and it was right out in plain sight. I could take the officers right upstairs and show it to them. It seemed, however, that this was no solution either. They could not enter her room without a search warrant, even if I admitted them. They could not get a search warrant because I had conducted an illegal search by entering the room looking for the drug. Even if they could get a warrant, possession of a small amount of marijuana is only a misdemeanor in the state of Michigan. Warrants for misdemeanors required three or four days to process. By that time she would surely have disposed of the evidence, and getting a warrant would have been a waste of time. In either case, it would have been no help for the immediate problem of retaining some vestige of order and control of The Next Door.

Even though Jackie didn't know that I could not have her arrested for possession of pot, she had already spread the word that I couldn't kick her out of The Next Door. Half the neighborhood was gathering in front of the house to cheer her victory. Since I was the personification of authority toward which their jeers were directed, and I was powerless to do anything, I went home. I had already stayed two hours late as it was, and Sharon and Nico were better able to effect calm and quiet than I.

The next morning I arrived at work to find marijuana smoke wafting out the upstairs bedroom window and my office door jimmied open. There was some minor vandalism, nothing missing. Once more I called the police. I had no special training for detecting marijuana smoke, and my expertise for purposes of obtaining a warrant was suspect. Though Jackie was an expert picker of locks, there was no concrete evidence for a charge of breaking and entering my office. Her fingerprints would be all over the office anyhow, because she had access to it during the daytime. Besides that, it would be analogous to charging someone with breaking into her own bathroom, since she lived there!

I calmly cleaned up the mess in my office, locked the door again, and set off to see a lawyer about obtaining eviction papers. The lawyer did not think he could effect an eviction procedure because Jackie had never paid any rent! His suggestion was that I execute a self-help eviction. I was to wait until she left the premises, then move her belongings out into the street, and lock her out of the house. Then if she tried to force her way in, I could call the police and it would be up to her to prove that she lived there and had a right to be inside.

The main difficulty with this strategy was that if any of the other residents let her back in, I would be right back where I started. In fact, the lawyer said, if any resident invited anyone else in as a guest and stated to the police that the guest was invited, the guest could not be arrested for trespassing. If Jackie and the other residents found out that they could invite into the house anyone they liked and I was powerless to get rid of anybody, the possibilities were staggering. They could party for days on end, or even start a commune in the attic!

I returned to the youth ministry, went to the executive director's office in the basement of The Open Door, and had a good cry. Being director of The Next Door was the first important job I had ever held, and in less than six weeks I had completely lost control of it. I couldn't figure out how to get Jackie to leave short of burning the house down. Dan was the executive director, and he could remember the days when narcotics officers prowled the drop-in center and the staff worried about being forced to testify against the guests in court. To him the situation was funny. "Don't worry," he said. "Things will work out. Look at it this way. On the one hand they're telling us that we are obliged to offer shelter to anyone who happens to walk in the door. On the other hand, they're telling us they can't do anything about any kind of illegal activities that go on inside the house. We could forget all this religion business and open a dope den. We'd make a lot more money!"

His humor helped me to reassess the situation. Jackie didn't know that I could not have her arrested for using marijuana. Neither she nor anyone else knew that if any resident had a guest, the police would not assist me in requiring the guest to leave. I decided to announce that The Next Door was not accepting any new residents until our legal problems were resolved, and to walk around looking smug and confident as if I knew exactly what I was going to do next.

I neither tried, nor needed to try, to bluff Jackie. By that time she had packed her belongings and was cleaning her room in preparation for moving out. It was amazing! Nobody else ever cleaned her room when she moved out. I didn't say much to Jackie, and she didn't say much to me. She left nonchalantly and with a great deal of dignity. The entire episode ended like a chess game I had unwittingly forfeited in my opening moves. For all I learned from that unequivocal but sporting checkmate, I am very grateful.

The first and most important thing I learned was that we could not provide shelter for people without cooperation on their part. Never again would I make or imply a unilateral promise to let someone stay at The Next Door indefinitely or unconditionally. That kind of promise was not only impossible to fulfill, but it was too much of an emotional issue. It made The Next Door symbolic of unfortunate situations in the girl's past against which she felt deep and bitter resentment. Out of all her past rejection arose behavior which paradoxically demonstrated what she most dreaded, namely that no one could love her. Because we so much wanted to provide a home for Jackie, our rejection of her was all the more humiliating and painful. This surely contributed to the lengths to which she was willing to go to challenge our right to make her leave.

Secondly, I learned that we had to be absolutely serious about our rules. Those rules were the minimal expectations we deemed necessary for safety, decency, and conviviality. If a person did not want to stay at The Next Door badly enough to follow them, she was probably not motivated to do other things that would be necessary to improve her life situation. If she did not comply with the rules during the first two weeks of residence, the chances of her improving her behavior during a longer visit were very slim. If she did not respect us on the staff enough to cooperate with our wishes in household matters, she probably would not respect anything we said in counseling sessions or evangelism.

Finally, I learned not to use punishment to maintain conviviality. When I gave Jackie extra chores to do, required an early curfew, and finally resorted to making her leave for short periods, I had only escalated her contempt for authority. I had also added to the number of dictates I was obliged to enforce until enforcement became impossible. It was absurd to treat someone progressively worse and expect her to behave progressively better.

Thereafter, when someone violated our rules, I had a frank but pleasant talk with her in my office. I explained the reason for the rule and the necessity for her cooperation. I listened to the reasons and excuses and made every possible accommodation to increase the probability that she would comply in the future. I assured her that we wanted her to stay at The Next Door and believed in her ability to do what was necessary to permit that to happen. Sometimes, if the rule was not one that involved the safety of other people, I repeated this routine two or three times with increasing emphasis on the necessity for her to comply if she were to stay longer. After two or three warnings, I asked her in the friendliest possible way to leave. I looked her straight in the eye, was very calm and not hostile or angry about it. I told her that if she left without a fuss The Next Door would be available to her if she needed it in the future. I did this early in the day so as to give her time to make other arrangements for the night. I let her use the telephone and gave her time to pack her belongings and exit with some vestige of dignity. I never had to call the police to get anyone to leave The Next Door again.

No one who was invited to leave, even in this kindly manner, took it as a gesture of friendliness. Each one took it as punishment and rejection. My assurance that I still cared about her as a human being and hoped the best for her made very little difference at the time. It was very small comfort that I was still willing to offer her counseling. Her immediate problem was to find a roof over her head for the following night. I never asked anyone to leave without seeing the pain and fear in her eyes and knowing the humiliation and danger to which she might be subjected.

I hated the idea that I was essentially using the offer of shelter as a contingency by which to control people. Carl Jung is quoted as saying, "Where love rules, there is no will to power." I believed then and still believe that real love does not insist upon control. At the same time, the responsibility of deciding what was acceptable or unacceptable behavior at The Next Door rested squarely on my shoulders. There was no escaping the role of authority and the necessity for controlling what people did while they were there. To make that control effective, I had to retain the power to withdraw the offer of shelter. Moreover, I had to use that power early and swiftly if I were to retain it, because there were no reinforcements if that power were chal-lenged. As an authority figure, I had to learn to live and work in the tension between love and control.

Our rules were as few and simple as we could make them. The only issues were safety, decency and conviviality. The most important rule was against smoking in the bedrooms upstairs. The point was not that smoking is a health hazard and an unnecessary expense. Nine out of ten of our residents smoked cigarettes and trying to prevent that would have taken all of our time and energy. But if a resident smoked in bed, she was endangering the lives of everyone else in the house. We could not monitor the bedrooms all night long, so we had to rely on voluntary cooperation and on guests monitoring each other. Each guest was instructed about the danger. If any guest caught another smoking upstairs, even during the day, she was to ask the person to take the cigarette downstairs immediately. If the smoker did not comply, the other guest was to inform the staff

right away. If cigarette butts were found in the bedroom, everyone in the room might be asked to leave. There were no second
chances on this rule. Enforcement was harsh, but absolutely
necessary for safety.

We also could not permit guests to have weapons, drugs,
alcohol, or pets on the premises, nor to engage in violent behavior or sexual activity. The degree of threat or blatancy was the
criterion for asking people to leave immediately if they broke
these rules, or issuing a firm warning. Keeping a knife under
one's pillow at night was quite different from threatening someone with it. Excessive petting on the living room couch was a
different matter from sneaking a boyfriend upstairs after hours.
In the case of drugs and alcohol, I would have preferred that the
girls not use them at all. Although I could determine with a fair
degree of accuracy whether they had been using them, I couldn't
prove it unless the substance was in their possession. We did not
sniff residents' breath when they came in at night, or examine
their eyeballs or search through their belongings. If they were
discreet enough to hide their use of drugs or alcohol effectively
and their behavior was not disruptive, they could, in effect, get
away with it. It was not my concern to police their actions, but
to maintain a healthy environment at The Next Door. Of course
I didn't tell them that.

There were a series of rules that existed for the sake of
comfort and convenience, regarding the use of the telephone
and the laundry, getting up at a reasonable hour in the morning,
helping to keep the house clean, and coming in for the night at
a specified time and being quiet so that everyone could get a
decent amount of sleep. We preferred that residents not have
visitors or watch television during the daytime hours. When we
had a house full of people, just sitting around talking or watching television, nobody accomplished anything. The house was
smoky and noisy, there were conflicts among people, and nobody had any privacy. I frequently made exceptions to these
rules. When someone was sick, I let her watch television during

the day if she wanted to. If there was a good reason for a long distance telephone call or a daytime visitor, she needed only to ask.

Late in my tenure as director, the Seinens and I came to an agreement not to allow residents to play radios and stereo sets. One reason was the noise level. When loud music was played, people needed to talk louder to be heard over it, and then someone else turned the music up even louder to be heard over the voices. The noise level seemed to affect people like a stimulant, and their hostility levels would rise with the increased decibels. Sometimes fights would ensue. Hour after hour of noise and tension wearied us and gave us headaches. More important than that, the words to much of the rock music they were playing extolled drugs, violence, illicit sex, and even Satanism. Each and every resident said she never paid any attention to the words. This, we felt, was more dangerous than if the words were clearly understood, because they seeped into the unconscious mind uncensored. Very frequently when I pressed one of the guests to tell me what she really believed about a situation, she would quote a line from a popular piece of music that she was unaware of having learned. If the environment were to be Christian we could not have destructive mythology reverberating between the walls. The Seinens did not want their children constantly bombarded by auditory trash. Not all rock music contained these degenerate messages, but we could not listen to each piece of music to evaluate it. Of course the women disagreed heartily with this rule and felt that it infringed upon their personal freedom. We stood firm, hoping that a few weeks of abstinence would have a quieting effect on their minds, would make them aware of the poetry to which they habitually listened, and perhaps even would cause them to be occasionally critical of it. The Seinens had a stereo on which they played instrumental and inspirational music in the evenings, which provided more convivial subliminal messages.

I had a special formula for eliciting voluntary cooperation

with our rules: Make a request, give a reason, and expect cooperation. The clearest example is the procedure for persuading
an uninvited daytime visitor to leave with the least possible fuss.
It was important not to confront the person with an accusation
that made him feel guilty. The fact was that he was already there
and probably knew that he should not be. Pointing that out to
someone who was homeless and unwelcome virtually anywhere
merely raised his defenses. We focused, instead, on what we
wanted him to do, namely leave, and stated that in the form of
a request. Giving a reason treated the person as a rational
human being. I read a short news item in *Psychology Today*[1] a long
time ago that reported research that showed that people respond to requests more consistently if they are given a reason.
It doesn't matter if the reason explains nothing or is patently
meaningless; it matters only that it is given. Finally, communicating the expectation of compliance permitted the individual
to leave without loss of face and feeling good about himself for
cooperating. The sequence of the three parts of the formula did
not matter; the trick was to include all three. I usually said
something like, "I would really appreciate it if you would be on
your way soon, because we don't usually have visitors here
during the daytime." "Be on your way" was a gentle way of
saying what I wanted him to do. The clause at the end sounded
enough like a reason to encourage rational behavior. The words
"appreciate" and "soon" gave him an opportunity to do something that would please me. Seventy-five per cent of the time,
the reply would be, "Oh, okay," and I would smile and walk
away. If I stood there with my arms folded and waited for him
to comply, I invited defiance.

When the formula did not work in a reasonable amount of
time, I simply repeated it, even more pleasantly and more imag-
inatively. If he was having a cigarette, a cup of coffee, or a
lingering conversation with his girlfriend, I might join him by
sitting down. This either gave him a couple of minutes of feeling
welcome, which was often all he wanted, or made the intimacy

a bit strained. Then I would casually say, "Well, as soon as you finish your cigarette, it's time for you to leave because we have a policy about that. I really appreciate your being so under-standing." And I would walk away again. If I had to approach him a third time, I usually needed only to smile. He would say, "I know. You want me to leave." I gave him a big congratulatory smile and he would go very soon.

The R. R. E. formula—request, reasoning, expectation—worked an overwhelming portion of times for all kinds of things such as getting the guests to be quiet, to do their chores, to come in on time at night, and not to leave empty pans to scorch on the stove. In fact, when I read the sheet of rules to them when they arrived, I used that formula, and when I had my little chats with them after they had broken rules I used it.

In the relatively small portion of times when it did not work, I used a variation of it that I called my "two-ton pillow ap-proach." I became very soft and comforting with voice tone and general demeanor, very heavy in my insistence, and practically inexorable. If I wanted someone to leave, I sat down beside him and mirrored his breathing, his posture and reflected his feel-ings very sympathetically. I spoke very softly, almost hypnotical-ly. As he began to fall into rhythm with my breathing and posture, I invited him with my body to stand up. I divided my request into smaller steps, if necessary, to effect standing up. I might say, "Do you know the name of that guy who just walked by on the sidewalk? Could you please have a look, because I'd really like to know." I stood at the same moment when he stood, and gently crowded him toward the door. Sometimes I put my arm around him and gently nudged him step by step, still listening or talking very compassionately. When we reached the door, I would invite him to return at a different time or encour-age him to set out for another specific destination. I surrounded and enveloped him in acceptance and loved him out the door. Then I went back into my office and collapsed from the effort!

The only time I remember the system not working was when

I was trying to persuade a very passive guest to wash the dishes. She had been there three days and had yet to do a single chore. I must have spent at least an hour establishing rapport. I loved her out into the kitchen and made moves to help her. Usually when I began a chore with someone, she would take over after I had moved a couple of coffee cups, but not this lady! I paced and matched every move she made and encouraged every step of the way. The minute I was interrupted by a phone call, she slipped back into the living room and lit up another cigarette. All day, off and on, I cajoled, badgered, and clowned, trying to get her to wash those dishes, and finally left for the evening with them still undone. Sharon said she would work on it. The next morning when I walked in, the dishes were in the sink and the water absolutely reeked. Sharon had been firmer than , and orderd her to do them. She had puttered a bit, gagged, and deliberately vomited in the dishwater. I was furious! "You get your body down here and wash those dishes," I yelled at her, "or you pack your bags and leave here right away!" She washed them, but it was the only task she did while she was there. She didn't cause any other trouble and I felt silly putting her out on the street because she wouldn't do chores. I ignored the undone tasks or did them myself, and terminated her stay at the end of two weeks. I had neither the time nor the patience to use the two-ton pillow approach on a resident more than once!

I really believe that the main reason so many of the women found it so difficult to cooperate at a basic level was their past experience with abusive authority. Nearly all had been physically and psychologically abused by parents, and many had been sexually abused. As children they needed authority figures to protect them and to help them grow. Instead, their authority figures overcontrolled them, punished unreasonably and irrationally, and left them with huge burdens of guilt, shame, anguish, and rage. Not only did they treat any authority with contempt, they also had no hope that any amount of cooperation on their part would prevent mistreatment. Our best hope for eliciting voluntary cooperation with minimal standards of conviviality was to be a different kind of authority than they had known in their pasts. They were far more likely to comply with our simple rules if they were convinced, first of all, that we loved them.

We went to great lengths to communicate that message to them. Just giving them a place to stay was not enough. It was important to smile when we greeted them, to take time to ask about their concerns, and to talk with them pleasantly. We complimented and thanked them for everything we could think of. These little exercises helped also to generate affection in us. We touched them whenever we could find opportunities to do so that seemed natural and appropriate. We took hold of their hands, we touched their shoulders, we hugged them whenever we could, even if they were sick or smelled bad. A behavioral psychologist would say that the best way to eliminate an unde-sirable behavior is to withdraw reinforcement of it. Most don't mention that reinforcement must have been offered at least a half-dozen times before the subject knows that there is anything to be withdrawn.

We avoided situations that gave the girls reasons to think we didn't like them. Sometimes a parent or a social worker would bring a young woman to The Next Door after an experience of extreme unpleasantness. I never left her sitting outside my office while I listened first to the people who were angry with her. She had a right to know what I was being told. If she didn't know, she imagined the worst. It was she with whom I had to get along, not the parent or the social worker. The basis for authority had to be trust, and she would not trust someone she believed did not like her. If she thought I couldn't possibly like her, she could stay up all night inventing ways to get even with me for that imagined dislike, and make my life absolutely miserable.

When the parent or social worker insisted upon venting her frustration to me in the presence of the guest, I listened carefully and empathically. I also took notes. The notes reflected my perception of what was being said from the girl's point of view.

They might contain such statements as, "It sounds as if Janie gets blamed for everything that goes wrong in the family." Sometimes I even wrote a note to her. "Dear Janie," it began. "If you have any spunk at all, you will read this when I leave the room to see your mother out the door. I want you to know that nothing she is saying is making me angry with you. As soon as she leaves, you and I will begin completely from scratch. You can tell me your side of the story and I will believe you. Love, Bobbie." When the parent was ready to leave, I laid the pad on the desk and left Janie alone in the office while I saw the parent out the door. If I returned to find her grinning and giggling at me, we were off to a fine start. If she hadn't read it, I didn't want to encourage her to read other people's private papers, so I ceremoniously tore it up and said, "Whew, I'm glad that's over. It must have been awful for you. Let's forget it and start all over."

Even if they didn't find out about that, parents often felt that I undermined their authority and let their daughters do whatever they wanted to do. Their authority, however, had been undermined in the first place, or they wouldn't have brought her to me. The only way I could establish my own authority was to disassociate it from the authority of the past. I never met a single girl or young woman who did not want to go home, who did not want to re-establish a relationship with her parents. The speed with which she came to that realization increased if she were not pressured to do that. She would do whatever she wanted to do in any case, at The Next Door or elsewhere. The probability of her wanting to do what I wanted her to do increased astronomically when she was convinced that I liked her, and believed there was a good chance that I might come to love her.

Sharon and Nico and the whole staff really tried to love people, and each of us had our own little helps for doing so. We generally tended to love people who presented us with opportunities to help them. Just knowing at the first meeting that a girl had endured unimaginable suffering engendered feelings of tenderness and affection. When we were physically tired, uncomfortable, emotionally spent, and thought we couldn't handle one more person with a problem, we would glance over at the cross hanging on the wall in the office. "Okay," we would say to the One who hung on it, "if all you're asking in exchange for that is to take care of one more person, we'll do it for you."

Everyone needed love. Nearly all would bend over backward to cooperate if they believed there was a chance of holding onto it. The offer of love was an even more powerful contingency in a person's life than shelter. Love is a prerequisite for conviviality and makes conviviality possible even when there is no safety, comfort, and general well-being. In the final analysis, love was the only power we had.

NOTES

[1]Langer, Ellen, Harvard University, Cambridge, Mass. 02138, and Arthur Blank and Benzion Chanowitz, City University of New York Graduate School and University Center, New York, N.Y. 10036. Cited in *Psychology Today,* Vol. 12, No. 9 (February, 1979), p. 28.

Chapter Five

Violence and Mercy

Violence is a fact of life in our society. During my childhood and the early years of my marriage I was able to pretend that it could only happen to other people or on television. The nightmare described in the first chapter, however, changed all that, and made me realize that I was at risk even in my own home. No one ever fired a gun in my direction in six and a half years at The Next Door. In that same time period, gunfire narrowly missed me twice in or around my suburban home: Once when I came upon a woman standing in her front yard shooting squirrels, and another time late at night when neighborhood teenagers playing with an air pellet gun accidentally fired through my bedroom window. Even though these guns were not aimed to shoot me, the threat was real. The illegality of discharging firearms within city limits offered me no protection at all.

Violence around the youth ministry was most frequently directed against property in the form of vandalism. When persons were the target, fists, blunt objects, or knives were used as weapons more often than guns. It was disturbing and frightening primarily because it was intentional in its destructiveness. My thinking about intentionality in violence is the product of my encounter with a young woman I'll call Babe.

The woman who gave birth to Babe was a patient in the back ward of a state mental institution. The child was placed in the custody of an aunt, who was probably as psychotic as the mother. Despite considerable physical and emotional abuse, Babe survived to the age of ten as a fairly normal black child who loved bubble gum, comic books, and an uninhibited female cousin who was a few years older than she. One afternoon while the aunt was away, the cousin was intimately fooling around with the boy next door. Babe was the lookout, seated on the bathroom floor chewing bubble gum and reading a comic book, her feet propped up against the door while the other kids were having at it in the same room. The aunt returned home, banged on the door and tried to force it open. Babe held the door as long as she could. When the aunt finally barged in, she was carrying a loaded gun. The cousin fled. Babe sat paralyzed with fear while the boy next door pled for his life for fifteen minutes before the aunt shot him. Babe watched him die on the bathroom floor.

The police came. The aunt told them that the boy was raping her daughter, that the shooting was an impulsive, unpremeditated act, that she had gone temporarily insane. Babe corroborated the story under threat of a similar fate. The aunt spent a few months in a mental hospital, and then was released to resume taking care of the children.

I met Babe soon after I began volunteering at The Next Door. She was seventeen, a tall, powerful young woman with an intense charismatic presence even when she was stoned out of her mind. She was violent at times, both destructive to property and assaultive. At other times she wrote very moving poetry, some of which was quite good. She told her story in horrible, colorful detail, and would sit on my lap like a small child and be comforted. She never lied. Sometimes she would refuse to discuss things, but she never lied. She had scars all over her body, some from early abuse, some from fights, and some from self-inflicted wounds. The scars and her willingness to let me comfort her elicited the emotional bond with her which ultimately outlasted the violence. I loved her very much.

When I became director of The Next Door, my role in her mind changed from that of a friend to that of an authority figure. I couldn't let her hang around all day and become involved with the daily affairs of the residents. That spelled rejection to Babe and I suddenly became the target of all her rage against authority figures. She slashed tires on my car, dumped several pounds of laundry detergent around the back entrance to my office, scribbled obscenities on the back door, broke into my files, and made threatening phone calls to my home which scared my kids terribly. She was very skilled at letting me know that she was the culprit without leaving evidence by which she could be caught and legally convicted. Several other people in the neighborhood who had reasons of their own for being angry with me joined forces with Babe. The battle lines seemed to be drawn over whether The Next Door was their turf or mine. Rumor had it that the goal was to keep up the harassment until I quit my job. This, given my commitment, was tantamount to a threat on my life.

One afternoon Babe confronted me about what she considered to be unfair treatment of another resident. I couldn't explain my position without violating a confidence. When I did not back down, she signaled two of her cohorts outside, who kicked down the obscenity-marred back door as well as the rotten doorjamb to which it was bolt locked. They tore through the house like a tornado, leaving overturned furniture, plants, ashtrays, and broken dishes strewn in their wake. On her way out Babe delivered a karate-like blow that broke in half the wooden sign that hung above the front porch. It all happened so quickly that I couldn't do anything to stop it.

The police arrived quickly and were very polite. They wondered why I let her come around to talk with me. "It doesn't look as though she actually did any damage," they said at last. "She just made a mess. You won't get very far prosecuting her for breaking a ten-cent coffee mug."

I asked about the door and the sign. From where I had been standing, I could not actually see either the kick that demolished the door or the blow that destroyed the sign. I had only heard the impact and seen the aftermath, which is circumstantial evidence.

Until then I believed that the Christian approach as well as the best strategy for stopping the harassment was not to reject Babe, but to forgive her just one more time. I was running out of cheeks to turn and my nerves were getting raw. I looked into having my phones tapped, to stop the calls to my home. It would have taken weeks or months to do it legally. I started a false rumor that the calls were being monitored, and they stopped immediately. Dan, then the executive director, arranged a warrant for Babe's arrest on a charge of malicious destruction of property through the prosecuting attorney's office without the help of the police. It took a week or more for the warrant to be served. Meanwhile I developed a system for hiding my car in several different places within a mile radius of the youth ministry, so that if I were followed back to my car at the end of the day it couldn't be found there the next. Each day I weighed the risk of driving my car to The Next Door against the risk of being assaulted while walking there.

One morning while hiding my car, I came to a red light and failed to see the sign that read, "No turn on red." Seconds before the light changed to green, I made a right turn. A police car appeared behind me, and its red light began flashing. I didn't even know what I had done wrong until the officer told me. That was the first time in the whole ordeal when I became really angry. "You can't do anything about my tires being slashed!" I shrieked at the policemen. "You can't do anything about my door being kicked down and my office being ransacked or threatening phone calls to my kids when I'm not home. I have to hide my car and I'm afraid of being beaten up on my way to work, and you can't do anything about any of it until after the fact. But I go through a niggling red light, and you give me a ticket! You know what I feel like doing? I feel like going down to the police station and overturning plants and ashtrays and furniture. Decently and in order, so I don't do any damage. But I'll bet you'd find some charge on which you could arrest me!"

"Yes, ma'am," said the puzzled officer, inexorably writing the ticket. "We surely would. And I could cite you for threatening an officer as well, so I'd suggest you calm down."

At last I understood Babe's rage against authority figures. Terrible injustices happen, and the police shake their heads politely. Judges believe lies and declare the truth inadmissable as evidence. But if the victim commits the slightest infraction, the weight of the law descends in full force. Like Babe, I repressed my anger toward the loved one who threatened me with real danger, and directed my rage instead against an impersonal authority figure who accused me but offered me no protection.

Babe did not beat me up on my way to work. I suppose one could say that I was protected by love. Several years later she admitted that she had intended to do it. I asked her why she didn't. "I knew what you'd do," she said. "You'd just stand there and let me do it, and then you'd look at me with big tears in your eyes and ask me why I was doing it. I just couldn't deal with that."

She was right. Throughout the three-month seige of Babe's destructiveness, I never felt really angry toward her. I felt hurt and bewildered, but not angry. When I was frightened I rehearsed in my mind the passive tactics of civil rights marchers and war protestors of the sixties. One agonizing question hung over my mind the entire time. I was willing in every cell of my conscious being to share Babe's suffering, to listen and understand as well as I was able and to give any kind of comfort I had in me to give. Still, she found it necessary to force her suffering on me in the form of physical violence. Why?

Throughout the entire time I knew Babe it always seemed to me that she was on the brink of conversion. Even during the worst of the violence, she would maintain a friendship with one or more individuals on the staff who felt compelled to plead with the rest of us for patience and lenience. When the tolerance of one wore thin, she moved on to another. Each of us experienced her charisma. Though she rarely spoke of anything religious, she consistently evoked from us the best sermons we ever preached. In our relationships with her we experienced amazing insights into our own lives and faith, as if God were using her to teach us. Never mind that we would arrive at staff meetings starry-eyed and hopeful about a conversation we just had with her, only to have her lob a brick through a window before the meeting ended! It was as if the Hound of Heaven pursued her wherever she went and wouldn't give up on her no matter what she did. Crazy as it may seem in retrospect, it was obvious at the time that she was one of God's chosen.

With the help of the warrant from the prosecuting attorney's office, Dan finally convinced her to stay away from The Open Door and The Next Door until the case came up in court nearly a year later. That meant that a year later we'd testify about the coffee mug, but we'd still care about her and would somehow find the grace to welcome her back with open arms when the case was resolved. We never prayed so fervently for anyone's conversion as we did for hers in that year!

When she returned, she was no longer violent. She was pregnant. It was a difficult pregnancy. Someone persuaded her to make a deal with God that if the baby were healthy, she would commit her life to Christ. I would never have suggested anything that risky because I had reasons to fear that there might be birth defects. Miraculously, Babe gave birth to a beautiful little girl who is bright and whole and healthy and has the same vibrant light in her eyes as her mother. Babe aligned herself with a Christian Reformed communal household in another city after the birth. She works part time and takes excellent care of her daughter. Several times a year she returns to Kalamazoo to visit relatives, and she and I make a point of spending time together. We are friends and I have permission to tell her story.

The societal factors which contribute to lawlessness and violence are varied and complex. Authority must be perceived as benevolent and just if people are to comply with its dictates voluntarily. The high rate of domestic violence alone is sufficient to emasculate respect for authority in this country, and to overwhelm the powers of the legal justice system to punish effectively. This society can no longer afford to allow its children to be abused or to rely primarily on punishment to preserve order and safety.

Not all criminals claim to have been abused as children, and many who were abused might have committed crimes if they hadn't been abused. Unfortunately, the principle "What goes around comes around" does not apply to acts of kindness and mercy. Everything I did at The Next Door which was in the least aversive to people was thrown back in my face or passed on to others several times over. Most of the things I did which were needed and enjoyed were not even appreciated, much less returned or passed on. It dawned on me one day during one of our prayer times that none of us, sinful creatures that we are, comprehends more than a small fraction of the blessings God showers upon us. Only the very devout even tithe in passing on to others the goodness and wealth we're aware of. But we take injury or misfortune very personally. We harbor guilt and resentment that take root in our lives and multiply themselves ten times over. We can't get rid of guilt and resentment ourselves, and we pass them on in ways we don't even realize. There is not now nor has there ever been enough goodwill on earth to right all the wrongs or to heal all the ills of humanity. This must come from Above. Only the sacrifice of one who is absolutely innocent can absorb our rage against suffering. Only the cleansing sacrament can free us from guilt, blame, and resentment and prevent us from passing our suffering on to others.

It was a delusion to think that my willingness to share Babe's suffering could extinguish sin in her life. First, I could not feel what she felt until I had experienced some of the same injustice she had experienced. Secondly, I wasn't perfect, whole and innocent. The delusion was a blasphemous glamorization of my suffering. My suffering could be redemptive to others only when it pointed toward Christ's suffering, and redemptive to me only when it echoed his. My rage toward the police remitted when I acknowledged my own genuine guilt and remembered that Jesus didn't have police protection for his ministry either.

I think violence and suffering should be avoided whenever possible. There is plenty to go around without our seeking it out or aggravating it. Certainly it should not be invited by hostile confrontation, even in the name of Christ, nor by our pride in our authority nor in defense of our power. My primary strategy for avoiding hostile confrontations was a habit of chanting silently in my mind an African tune I learned many years ago. "Kyrie eleison, Christe eleison." The words sounded over and over. I didn't know much Greek or Latin, but I knew that I was calling down God's mercy both on myself and the angry person I was facing. Out of this chant evolved the two-ton pillow approach referred to earlier, almost without my thinking about it until after the fact. The chant inspired and reminded me to admit quickly and freely when I was wrong, which was effective in disarming hostility. This enhanced rather than diminished the respect the girls had for me by accommodating their need for justice.

There is a whole system for training human services workers called Confrontation Avoidance Techniques.[1] The principles are: 1. Intervene in a hostile situation as early as it is detected, before it escalates to the point of being out of control. 2. Don't intervene in an authoritarian way. Speak in a calm, quiet voice. Offer the hostile person an honorable and effective way to take care of his or her anger. Invite the person away from the situation. 3. Don't corner a hostile or angry person. If a person is positioned in a room relative to walls, furniture and doors in such a way that he or she must move toward you to get away from you, the person is cornered. This increases the probability of attack. 4. Relax. Relax facial muscles, neck and shoulder muscles, arm and hand muscles so that they telegraph neither fear nor anger. Appear completely calm and placid. 5. Though relaxed, mirror the angry person's body position. Sit at exactly the same moment he or she sits and stand up at the same time. If you sit down first, you tempt attack; if you stand over him or her, that's cornering. Though I didn't know about Confrontation Avoidance Techniques until after I left The Next Door, I used some of them intuitively. They would have been very useful, had they all been available to me.

Direct victimization was not the only impact of violence on the ministry. The fear of violence in other segments of the community affected us as well. A case in point was an incident of apparently random intentional violence which started a chain reaction that brought about several changes in our work.

About two years after I became the director of The Next Door, a young female entrepreneur selected a little storefront at the other end of Ranney Street for a clothing boutique. She worked several weeks preparing for its opening. Late one afternoon when she was alone in the store, two young men came in. They meant to rob her, but she had no money to speak of. One of the men left. The other beat her, raped her, tried to strangle her with a belt, and stabbed her. She was left unconscious and barely alive in the back room of the store. She regained consciousness and somehow summoned the strength to drag herself to the front of the store where she could attract someone's attention. Fortunately, help was quick in arriving. Before she was taken to the hospital, and though her pulse was too faint to detect, she gave the police a description of her assailants.

Within an hour or two, a young man was arrested for the assault. He was a resident in the state-operated halfway house for delinquent boys located at the other end of Ranney Street, right beside The Next Door. The staff on duty at the halfway house turned him in.

When I heard the story my first thought was that he could just as easily have walked into The Next Door as that little boutique. Not only did I frequently work alone both during the day and during the evening, but Sharon and Nico and their sons, my volunteers, or any of our guests could have been the victims.

Before I could even begin to think of ways we could protect ourselves, the whole ministry was threatened by the community's response to violence. Some of the people who lived on Ranney Street or came there regularly, shocked by the brutality of this incident, blamed the concentration of halfway houses in the neighborhood. They included The Open Door and The Next Door in their blame, even though they weren't technically halfway houses. Some of the people who felt most strongly about this had even used our services. The state halfway house received a telephone call threatening that all three houses would be fire-bombed if they weren't immediately closed down. What a way to make the neighborhood safer! We had to take the threat seriously. The police could do little except patrol the street more frequently and warn us to watch out. The newspaper withheld the story for a few days so as not to call attention to the threat and increase the probability of its being carried out.

We waited and watched for three days. Then we heard of a petition being circulated demanding that the city commission act to remove all of the halfway houses in the neighborhood. The city commission had no controls over us except through zoning ordinances and building codes. In order to discourage violent tactics against us, the news media released the story about the petition, contrasting it with the earlier threats and giving it some credibility. Headlines on page one of the paper and on-site television coverage attracted a great deal of public attention to the ministry, which was a mixed blessing.

Every city, county, or state bureaucrat who had the remotest connection with us wanted to make sure that no technicality under his or her jurisdiction was out of order. The building inspector paid a call, inspected the houses, and ordered us to install railings on the porch steps within thirty days. The zoning ordinances were checked, and we were found to be within those limitations. An official from the state department of social services took a close look at our license to shelter juveniles, and came to visit.

It was the responsibility of the state department of social

services to ensure the safety and appropriateness of facilities offered to shelter juveniles. When The Next Door opened, there were no other facilities for runaway teenagers or for kids whose parents put them out of their homes. The state then was willing to allow The Next Door to shelter juveniles with a license like that of any private individual who was willing to undertake foster care. Maintenance of this license required an annual physical examination for the houseparents and an inspection to determine that we had enough beds and space for the number of people living there. With this license and a signed statement of permission from a parent or guardian within twenty-four hours of a girl's arrival, we could care for her. Minors seventeen and older in Michigan are not prosecuted for status offenses such as running away or truancy, so we could accept them with or without a license and parental consent.

In the intervening years, federal, state and local funding had offered the community another shelter for runaways. Its location, remote from the downtown street scene, reduced exposure to drugs and other unsavory aspects of street life. The other shelter had a larger staff for closer supervision and for working with runaways and their families. I referred every girl I could to them. When their beds were full or a girl didn't fit into their guidelines, they made referrals to me.

Compared with the other shelter, and in the light of the publicity we received, The Next Door was no longer considered by the state to be safe or appropriate for teenagers. When girls stayed at The Next Door they were not at all times under the direct supervision of the houseparents, but in the care of the staff as a whole. Therefore we needed a group home license like that of the other shelter. A group home license entailed education and experience requirements of staff which we probably could have finagled somehow. A bigger problem was the requirement that group homes have fire doors, free-standing exterior fire escapes, and separately wired alarm systems. These improvements would have cost several thousand dollars, which the ministry didn't have, so sheltering juveniles suddenly became illegal.

All things considered, it probably was too risky to take girls younger than seventeen. But facing that fact was disappointing and embarrassing. We installed smoke alarms and escape ropes in the upstairs bedrooms after that.

A more positive aspect of the media attention that was focused on the ministry was the opportunity it gave us to explain what we believed and why we were there. We sent out a newsletter with an article entitled "Who Is My Neighbor?" which is the question Jesus was answering when he told the parable of the Good Samaritan. The article reviewed the attack on the woman in the boutique, the violent threats, and the protest petition. It both supported the efforts of the halfway house and differentiated the youth ministry from it. Then it continued:

> Ranney Street has always been a tough neighborhood in which to . . . attempt [to be a neighbor]. This recent incident is only the jagged tip of the proverbial iceberg of crime in this area. We can well understand the fears of older people and business people who favor the petition. Our resident counselors and houseparents live here too, and both staff and clients have been victims of theft, vandalism and minor assaults. We understand also the fears of residents who are young, poor, and transient, some of them former clients [of ours]. . . . They sign the petition as a way of crying out against a crime as violent as this.
>
> All of these, then, are our neighbors. We are still here for those who need shelter and food and for those who drop in for counseling, fellowship, coffee, aspirin, and band-aids. Now we are extending ourselves further in a house-to-house visitation, offering our services as peacemakers, offering understanding and cooperation in such things as trying to persuade people to make restitution for theft and vandalism. We'll even inspect apartments for security and help to install more effective locks for residents who need them.
>
> It is obvious that neither the neighborhood nor the city will necessarily be safer if the halfway house and the youth ministry should disappear. It is dangerous to leave people

cold and hungry on the streets. It is dangerous to lock people behind bars and do nothing to rehabilitate them. It is dangerous not to know our neighbors, because then help is unavailable in crises and emergencies. When hatred, fear, and violence exist in our community, we all bear the consequences, for we are all neighbors. "The world," to quote William Sloane Coffin, "is now too dangerous for anything but truth and too small for anything but love. We have to learn to be merciful because we are at each other's mercy."

The newspaper gave the article a half-page spread on the religion page under the headline, "Youth Ministry Promotes Mercy!"

One might be tempted to say that the entire episode turned out for the best. The woman who was attacked recovered, and the assailant was tried and convicted. Losing permission to shelter juveniles wasn't altogether unfortunate, and the ministry was able to make a public statement of its purpose. I am still unwilling to say that such a brutal incident as this was God's will. The concept of a God who is both omnipotent and merciful is still incompatible with the fact of violence, and human suffering remains a mystery. It is clear, however, that God's presence which we sought so fervently was imminent throughout our experiences. That presence enabled us to think fairly clearly, act without panic, extend ourselves to reach out to those who would be our enemies and find benefits from the situation both in the midst of it and in retrospect. The realization that we had been sustained through very bad times taught us to trust that God's Spirit would be with us in danger and safety, suffering and joy, as well as the daily work when it was tiring and boring.

I would not wish to leave the impression that episodes of violence such as I have described were usual or normative. We didn't keep records of violent incidents, but the best estimate of the average frequency is five or six incidents in or around both The Open Door and The Next Door in a year. This guess excludes the series of incidents during the first few months of my directorship of The Next Door, and includes deliberately broken windows, fights on the property, and assaults on staff members. None of the latter required hospitalization. One might well ask whether this amount of violence interfered with our effectiveness. On one hand, the time we spent replacing broken windows and quieting the fold after an outbreak of violence might have been spent counseling or teaching if the outbreaks could have been avoided. On the other hand, the Lord's work has always been done in the midst of the violent human condition and no place is really safe. It's impossible to evaluate the impact of our vulnerability and our response to violence on those who witnessed it. The rate and intensity of violence was not so high as to keep us constantly on edge and fearful, but had profound effects on our ministry.

Violence affected our public ministry through what we wrote and said to constituents. It was an affirmation of our commitment and a prophetic statement about the sorry state in which society finds itself. On one hand, part of our economic support was motivated by the hope that the ministry decreased the amount of violence in the community. On the other hand, there were people who might have been willing to volunteer their time if the ministry were not perceived as dangerous. Others found the degree of risk acceptable for an adventurous missionary effort in which they could participate for a few hours a week.

I am unaware of either paid or volunteer staff members leaving the ministry because of violence. We were accurately informed of the risks during orientation. Our foolish, saintly commitment to the ministry seemed to grow firmer with our awareness of God's presence in each incident we endured. Indeed it was that awareness of God's presence that made the difference between whether the outcome was ultimately constructive or destructive.

Our vulnerability greatly enhanced our commitment to each other. Our only protection against injury resulting either from direct hostility against us or from random outbreaks of suppressed rage was to look out for each other. The young men who worked at The Open Door made a habit of checking up on female staff who were working at The Next Door alone. The Next Door staff kept sensitive ears open for commotions at The Open Door so that we could be available as distractions, to help disperse a crowd, as peacemakers in calming people down, or as witnesses if push came to shove. No matter how vehement disagreements and personality clashes among the staff were, they were kept in perspective by the danger to which we were all subjected. There was simply no contest between our concerns with our individual ideologies and our concern for each other's hides!

The frequency of violence definitely affected our relationships with those we served. The best and primary approach to the problem of violence was preventive. The best preventive measures involved treating people with love and mercy. Of course we intended to treat people with love and mercy to begin with, but the subtle, ever-present threat of their acting out anger did keep us on our toes!

It's honest to say that we were far more afraid for our guests than we were afraid of them. They were subjected to greater risks than we were because they did not know how to avoid hostile confrontations. When they left us they often went into living situations that offered little protection from violence. Among approximately four hundred people with whom the ministry had contact in any given year, we heard of one or two deaths per year. This constitutes a mortality rate two or three times the national average for their age brackets. Some of the deaths were the results of intentional violence in the form of murder or suicide. Others resulted from accidents, and still others resulted from illnesses. Our consciousness of their fragility generated a sense of urgency in our work. Whether our first concern was for their physical bodies or for their immortal souls, we all tried to impress upon them our concern with patterns of behavior that appeared dangerous. We could not afford to leave warnings unspoken. Neither could we afford to leave words of love unspoken or acts of mercy undone. Lives and souls so precariously balanced between the abyss and the hand of the Almighty required the utmost tenderness.

In the park in downtown Kalamazoo is a lovely monument. Bronze statues of children stand or sit casually on pedestals placed in one end of a reflecting pool. Some are small, some are nearly grown; some are Caucasian, some are of other races. At the other end of the pool is an abstract monolith with a cascade of water flowing over it. In the pattern made by the water and sunlight can be glimpsed a prophetic figure watching over the children. The caption reads, "Where mercy and justice prevail, children may safely play."

NOTE

[1]Ditman, William, Ph.D. Waukegan Developmental Center, Waukegan, Illinois.

⟿ | *Chapter Six*

Intimate Tragedy

The first time I heard an account of the intimate tragedy of incest, I did not believe it. I thought the young woman who was reporting it was making it up. I thought she was ventilating an Oedipal fantasy of her childhood and manipulating the sympathies of counselors and social workers. I could not imagine that it was physically possible for an adult male to penetrate the body of a small child sexually. I could not imagine that it was humanly possible for a person who seemed to be in control of his mental faculties to abuse a child in that way. I could not imagine that family ties between the parents and between parents and children could remain in place in the face of violation of this taboo. The horrors of Nazi concentration camps were easier to incorporate into my view of what it means to be a member of the human race than was the prevalence of sexual abuse of children.

My experience in listening to other stories told me by the girls, some factual, some fictitious, was that those that sounded the most bizarre often turned out to be true. Instead of challenging the truthfulness of that first young woman, I asked questions. The more I listened, the more cohesive her story sounded. As she began to talk about it candidly in front of other residents, they chimed in, "Oh, that happened to me too!" Some had been molested by fathers or stepfathers, others by brothers, step-brothers, uncles, cousins, or acquaintances of the family. I still wondered if the stories were a symptom of a mental pathology they had somehow caught from each other, or if they were competing to blow my mind.

I began talking with counselors from other agencies, saying, "I seem to be up to my eyeballs in incest cases. Is there an epidemic going around?" Those who had been sensitized to the problem assured me that sexual abuse of children is indeed a problem of epidemic proportions. They suggested a few books for me to read on the subject, and suggested that I join the Child Abuse and Neglect Council.

The council was a voluntary organization of human services professionals and other interested citizens who coordinated services and initiated programs to prevent, stop, and mitigate the effects of many kinds of child abuse and neglect. The long-hidden horror of sexual abuse was at last claiming their attention. People were beginning to talk about it, and research was beginning to find its way into circulation. I worked with the Child Abuse and Neglect Council to determine the scope of the problem in our immediate community, to provide some training for professionals who were encountering it, and to develop some programs to deal with it. In the bargain, I received an education.

We defined sexual abuse as exploitation of a child's sexuality by an adult or someone in authority. This included physical contact such as vaginal, anal, or oral intercourse, attempted intercourse, or fondling. All of these are violations of Michigan's Criminal Sexual Conduct Code if the victim is under the age of sixteen. We also included acts that did not involve touching, such as exhibitionism, voyeurism, or verbal stimulation. Anything that involved a child sexually with an adult or someone who was significantly older or physically larger was considered detrimental to the child. A child does not have a choice in such matters because of the possibility of intimidation and threats.

Furthermore, a child is taught that adults are to be obeyed. Although violence occured in less than half of the cases that were reported, according to an extensive survey conducted in Chicago,[1] coercion was almost always an element. The same research showed that children are nearly always molested by people they know, at least a third by members of their own households. No significant differences in the frequency rates of sexual abuse were found when comparing various ethnic groups or socio-economic classes. These findings were consistent with research conducted in other parts of the country.

Victims, according to most available literature, seem to be at least twice as likely to be female as male. Perpetrators in reported cases are nearly always male. Perhaps it is possible for women who are taking care of children sometimes to stimulate children sexually under the guise of extreme hygienic measures, perhaps without even realizing it. This would be difficult to document because it is not identifiable as abuse. The victim, even as an adult, may not recognize it as an exploitation of his or her sexuality. It would, however, fall within the broad definition of the Child Abuse and Neglect Council.

The most shocking facts about sexual child abuse were the statistics indicating its prevalence. Various studies showed the rates of sexual abuse to be between sixty and eighty per cent among teenaged prostitutes, drug and alcohol abusers, female prisoners, and females seeking mental health services.[2] These figures corroborated inescapably the reports heard at The Next Door. Even more disturbing than those findings were the results of a retroactive survey among college-aged women in a normal population in which twenty-eight per cent reported sexual encounters with an adult prior to age thirteen.[3] Among my social acquaintances, so many women have spoken of such experiences that I do not doubt these figures. Nor can I walk into a grocery store or attend a meeting even in my own church without being haunted by the awareness of the probability that one out of every four women was sexually abused as a child.

Perhaps even more remarkable than the prevalence of sexual

child abuse is the fact that so many former victims live apparently productive and satisfying lives. Though they doubtless suffered
from emotional anguish and even psychological scarring, they
have resisted or avoided destructive patterns of thought and
behavior that would interfere with their ability to function as
adults. Some former victims I have known socially have used the
services of a psychotherapist at one or more times in their lives.
Most, however, have never been hospitalized for mental illness
nor become chronically disabled by it. They have not become
addicted to drugs or alcohol, committed crimes, or been in
trouble for sexual behavior. Heaven only knows what inner
strength is required for them to attend effectively to the daily
business of living, or where they find that strength. My guess
is that the human spirit is capable of overcoming even this
intimate tragedy.

I attended a workshop on sexual abuse sponsored by the
Michigan Division of the National Council on Alcoholism. I was
given a list of adolescent and adult problems which were indica-
tors of possible sexual abuse in childhood. Those problems were
typical of a majority of guests at The Next Door. Thereafter I
was inclined to be more tolerant and patient with them. Even
if sexual abuse existed only as a suspicion in my mind, I was
unable to be deeply angry with someone who might have been
raped as a child. As I heard more and more of their stories I
came to understand how they learned to feel and behave as they
did. Explanations, however, neither justify nor excuse destructive behavior. In retrospect, I think there were times when I
tolerated too much, and this was a disservice to the victims, to
the staff at The Next Door, and to myself. Given the inevitability
of errors in tolerance, I have fewer regrets for my excesses than
my deficiencies.

One notable common characteristic of former sexual abuse
victims given at the workshop was a preoccupation with other
people's feelings and needs, often to the neglect of their own.
I heard stories about role reversals with mothers in which mothers were sick, weak, or overworked, and the daughters took care

of them. Sexual abuse victims were often the eldest daughters
of their families, and were often charged with responsibility for
the household and for care of younger children in addition to
an adult sexual role. Many believed that their acquiescence
prevented the abuse of younger brothers and sisters. Sometimes, though, they discovered that younger siblings suffered
similar treatment. Even though the kind of self-sacrifice they
carried as habits into their adult lives was often destructive and
unhealthy, I found it deeply touching.

Many former victims seemed not to trust their own perceptions of reality. As children, they seemed to need to trust and
love the adults around them, and to believe what adults said
regardless of what they did. The hush imposed by perpetrators
at the time of the abuse forced the victim to repress her feelings
and contributed to her distrust of reality. Some detached themselves from events so completely that they convinced themselves that what happened was a bad dream or that it happened
to somebody else.

The incredulity of other people also contributed to victims'
sense of unreality. Many victims tried, despite threats and intimidation, to tell their secret. Children rarely bear false witness
about such matters because they risk so much in what they tell.
Still, most victims were disbelieved. I heard stories about mothers who surely closed their ears and eyes and denied any possibility of it. I heard stories about mothers who punished their
daughters for telling what sounded like filthy and terrible lies.
When reality was forbidden expression in words, it seemed not
to be true. The denial of others forced victims to suffer alone
and to struggle within themselves with their perceptions of what
was real.

A third common phenomenon among former victims involved unusual patterns of concentration. Compulsive concentration on virtually anything provided escape from painful and
forbidden feelings. Obsession with other people's feelings was
part of this pattern. More common at The Next Door was
inability to concentrate on anything for effective lengths of time.

Many of the girls, though apparently intelligent, seemed unable to pay attention to any task long enough to get it done. This may have been part of the problem of detachment described above. Another possibility is that in their learning years they were constantly distracted from play, schoolwork, and friendships by the secret which could not be told.

Needless to say, these abnormal concentration patterns would have created problems in school. Physical discomfort and unattended injuries accounted for part of the distraction from learning. Preoccupation with feelings of shame and anger might have accounted for longer lasting disruption of learning processes. Victims who were able to memorize information well enough to receive good grades suffered another kind of learning interruption: they were socially isolated and the information had little meaning for them. Both kinds of interruptions resulted in deficiencies in knowledge or in skills and added to their perception of themselves as failures in life.

Exposure to sexual activity at an early age was bound to affect attitudes toward sexuality in later life. As one might expect, some former victims of sexual abuse wanted nothing more than to avoid sexual contact. Several have told me that they felt that sexual abuse contributed to their inclination toward homosexuality. I was unable to substantiate this theory in any research I could find. Other victims became markedly seductive toward males and promiscuous at an early age. This response was often viewed by outsiders as a cause of early sexual exploitation rather than as a behavior pattern that was conditioned by it. Children have sexual feelings and are capable of being stimulated. If these feelings were exploited early on, one can easily see how sex might become a disproportionate preoccupation in later life. Regardless of how seductively a child might behave, she has a right to expect restraint and continence on the part of her elders. In the absence of such restraint, the child learns to expect sex in any and every relationship. A child who was bribed to be cooperative and secretive might have come to see sex as a powerful tool for getting anything she wanted. Many former victims of sexual abuse are afraid to refuse any sexual advances made toward them. Perhaps their helplessness led them to believe that they had no right to any choice in how their bodies were used. They may have been afraid that their families would fall apart or that they would lose everyone they loved if they resisted. This fear came true for a few when they reported the abuse to authorities and were removed from their homes and placed in foster care. It would have made much more sense to have asked the perpetrators to leave.

It seemed that sexual abuse in childhood increased the probability of subsequent victimization later in childhood and beyond. I remember a story about a little girl from an incestuous home who was raped by a man who sat beside her in a movie theater. A representative from the Sexual Assault Program in Kalamazoo estimated that seventy per cent of the women who sought help after being raped mentioned childhood sexual abuse. It is possible that victimization engenders an attitude of fear, helplessness, and subjugation which is communicated through body language to someone who is out looking for a victim. This attitude, if it exists, does not provoke an attack, but rather increases the probability of a former victim being chosen again. Since rape is a crime of violence rather than of passion and is not related to sexual attractiveness, it is unlikely that the tendency toward promiscuity mentioned above is a factor. (This theoretical explanation should never be used callously as an answer to a rape victim's poignant question, "Why me?")

Nearly all who experience exploitation of their sexuality in childhood feel that they must have done something which brought on their experience. A typical childlike world view is that bad things happen to bad people, that pain is the same as punishment. The same logic is operative in those who find fault with the victims. The belief in guilt keeps alive some semblance of faith in authority and in the rightness of the way things are in the world. It gives victims the illusion of control over what happened to them, albeit at the expense of their self-esteem. False guilt combined with anger was a factor in the high incidence of suicide attempts, self-mutilation, and psychosomatic illness among our young women.

Other factors contributed to the potential for self-destructiveness and an unintentional propensity to suffer. Some former victims were so detached from their feelings that they needed to prove to themselves that feeling pain was still possible. Others needed an acceptable reason to cry. Still others wanted to make those who had wronged them sorry for what had been done. I also suspected that any injury or illness in childhood which might have necessitated a trip to a hospital or doctor's office stopped abuse temporarily because of the threat of discovery. Physical injury or illness may also have elicited the kind of caring and concern for their bodies that these children needed and craved. Any of these factors taught former victims to seek pain as an improvement in their circumstances. The propensity toward self-injury, like the tendency toward promiscuity, is often misinterpreted as a cause of sexual abuse rather than as an effect.

Drug and alcohol abuse are closely associated with both general child abuse and sexual abuse of children. I have heard of men who both claim that they could not stop the abuse of their families because they were drunk, and yet claim that they drink because they cannot face their guilt in abuse. I have known of victims who used drugs and alcohol to escape from pain, and later found themselves in circumstances where they were unable to flee or defend themselves from rape because they were under the influence of alcohol or drugs. Many studies explore the relationship between the two phenomena.[4] A social profile of an incestuous family is similar to that of an alcoholic family. Families who have one or more members who are alcoholics suffer enough social stigma without adding the suspicion of incest to their burden. The overlapping of the problems, however, suggests the possibility of certain characteristics increasing the potential for both substance abuse and child abuse.[5]

A high-risk family has a rigid hierocratic structure of authority and domination. One person, usually the father, is designated to be the person who decides what is allowable and what is not. There may be some competition for this role between the parents, but the role itself is rigid in that it is assumed that there can only be one authority and that that authority is to be obeyed without question. Since obedience is to be unconditional, the standards for the authority are perfectionistic. There is no room for admission of error on the part of the authority, because this would call into question the right to be obeyed. Perfectionistic standards, since no one can live up to them, generate distrust. The authority figure, internally doubting his right to be obeyed, sees other family members as undermining his authority. When he is inconsistent or imperfect, the blame is projected onto those subject to his authority. Every failure in obedience threatens his position.

Each member of the family sees himself or herself as essentially bad. The distrust generates fears: fears of rejection, isolation, and punishment; fears that a fault or weakness will be discovered. These fears permit no freedom for the expression of feelings. Fear and anger cannot be shared openly, acknowledged, and accommodated because they threaten the family authority structure. Emotional needs must be accommodated through manipulation. Authority must be appeased and subjects must be hushed up.

Emotional bonds between family members are more likely to be based on fear of other family members or collusion against others than on affection. Perhaps a father and daughter would collude against a perfectionistic mother, or mother and son collude against the father's drinking and abuse. The parents are emotionally and sexually detached from each other, and looking to other members of the family for emotional support or to chemicals for comfort. Some members of the family are bound together because of their exclusive dependence on each other while others are excluded or rejected. All of this must be kept secret. Secretiveness and exclusivity intensify relationships and create dependencies.

Because fear is such a large factor, family members feel a

great need to control each other. The greater the fear and insecurity, the greater the need for control. Frightened, insecure, angry family members try to gain control through punishment. Their rebellious behavior threatens the family structure. This generates an escalating cycle. The more one relies on punishment for control, the more rebellion. The more rebellion and threat to authority, the greater the inclination to punish.

The more intense the cycle becomes, the greater the need for secrecy. No one must learn how frightened the authority figure is. No one must learn how shaky the structure is. No one must know of the secret alliances and the contempt that is felt toward others. No one must find out about the surreptitious strategies necessary for living through each day. No one must know that punishment fails to ensure control, or that it gets out of hand. The whole family is isolated from outsiders. There are no adult friends of the family who might offer some emotional support and relieve the need for dependency. There are no external influences against perfectionistic standards and excessive punishment.

This risky, closed family structure is as much a matter of concern to the Christian community at large as it was to us who attempted to do ministry at The Next Door. Not only did we find ourselves faced with the damage generated by this pattern of authority, we frequently found the pattern supported by a rigid, dogmatic set of beliefs disguised as Christianity. This belief system stressed the obedience of children without obliging the parents to be merciful and kind. It supported the father as unquestioned head of the household, answerable only to his private perception of God. It posed a code of conduct followed to perfection as the criterion for salvation. The fear of condemnation and punishment was seen as the primary motivating factor. Honest, direct expression of feelings was seen as evil. Control of relationships was all important, and the authority figure was responsible for controlling the actions of those in submission to him. Punishment was a divine right. The boundaries and authority of the isolated family were considered sacred.

Any interference was perceived as evil and to be resisted at all cost.

Incest is a historical taboo, but we find an instance of it reported in Genesis 19:30 ff. when Lot's daughters become pregnant by their father. It is interesting to note that excessive consumption of alcohol was a factor in this story as it commonly is in the modern phenomenon. In light of Lot's earlier willingness to hand over his virgin daughters to the mob intent upon carnal knowledge of his guests, and the practically universal tendency to blame the victims of rape and incest, one wonders if the story might have been told differently from a female perspective.

Clearly, this story did not find its way into our Scriptures as a model to be emulated, nor do the abuses of authority described above reflect the Christian ideal of family life. In our experience at The Next Door, theological arguments alone were insufficient to counter a girl's belief system, which permeated the intimate fabric of years of living. Our ministry required a way of exercising authority which contrasted with the closed system point-for-point. A model for authority more consistent with Christian beliefs was the Suffering Servant rather than the domineering patriarch. Wholeness rather than perfection was the goal.

An early task in our dealings with victims of the intimate tragedy was to replace fear with trust. To do this, it was first necessary for us to love them and to treat them with respect and good will. Years of fear and distrust could not be vanquished overnight. We had to be patient in assuring them that they were safe from condemnation with us, showing with our constancy that their secrets were safe. We had to teach them to express their feelings honestly, at first in such simple matters as preferences in food. By being straightforward and honest in expressing our own feelings, we helped them to learn constructive ways to express deeper feelings such as anguish, grief, and rage. We had to counter their detachment with compassion and empathy, and respond to their feelings no matter how trivial or how intense. We exercised a minimum of control over them and supported their decisions and their freedom of choice in every way that we could. We refrained from using punishment in favor of extensive efforts to elicit their voluntary cooperation. Only when we could demonstrate a different way of relating and living together in conviviality was it meaningful to try to teach them about the merciful God of Christianity.

I had no special clinical training for treating the psychological and emotional problems generated by sexual abuse. My strategies were simple ones that any well-meaning person who was sensitive to the problems could use. When I became aware of behavior and feelings that suggested sexual abuse, I said very matter-of-factly, "Many people who have the kind of problem you have were sexually abused as children." It was easier for them to talk about it if I brought up the subject than if I asked open-ended questions that required them to put it into words. Frequently the person welcomed the invitation to tell her story to someone who was willing to believe it, and felt comforted that the problem was not hers alone. If she denied it, I did not press the issue. I did not try to do intensive therapy to help them resolve their feelings quickly and dramatically. I simply listened with understanding. If someone's feelings seemed to be getting out of control, I gently steered her toward less intense aspects of the story, to easier parts of it over which she already had some control.

I wanted to be a different role model from the one our guests had experienced before. As a woman who had daughters nearly their ages, it would have been easy to assume a motherly role. This caused me two kinds of problems. One was extreme dependency. They would have preferred living the rest of their lives in a situation of protective, loving, comfortable care to learning to protect themselves, make their own decisions, and find comfort and caring in adult relationships. Occasionally they would do destructive things to themselves in order to be allowed to return to that kind of situation. A second problem was that they unconsciously fell into the manipulative, overly-adaptive roles they had learned to assume with their mothers, or acted out their resentment and rebellion against me. Therefore, I did not allow them to call me "Mom" and suggested instead that they think of me as a friend, an older sister, or an aunt. If they had been overly controlled and isolated as children, they needed to learn to think of authority less in terms of a monolithic, dominant power structure and more in terms of a human partnership.

A male in this situation had different kinds of problems. Former sexual assault victims tended to be fearful and resentful of men or to behave seductively toward them. Though Nico rarely became a father figure to the girls, he carried out a male authority role well. He was gentle and unobtrusive and never imposed his presence upon them. He was sensitive toward their feelings and their physical complaints, joked with them gently, and provided an excellent model for protectiveness and caring in his own family. He was embarrassed at times by seductive behavior which occasionally took the form of exhibitionism. Sharon and I had to remind guests who had never been per-mitted any personal privacy not to run around the house unclothed.

The most healing role a man can take with an abused woman is that of one who is sensitive, understanding and concerned but will not under any circumstances take sexual advantage of her. In church settings I have known many women who developed intense crushes on male clergy, and a shocking number of clergy who became sexually involved with them. In several of those instances with which I am familiar, I am also aware that the women were among the one out of four in the congregation who were sexually exploited as children. This, in my view, is but another form of incest, and I doubt that it would happen as frequently as it does if male clergy understood the nature of their attractiveness as authority figures.

In the New Testament, we find many examples of Jesus' compassion for women, even those caught in the act of adultery. I have a fantasy that He had a precise sensitivity to their feelings and life situations. My favorite story in which this fantasy is entwined is Jesus' encounter with the Samaritan woman in John 4. The Anchor Bible Commentary cites a Jewish document circa 65-66 A.D. in which Samaritan women were never to be trusted with ritual purity because they were menstruants from their cradle! My perhaps exaggerated sensitivity triggers the suspicion of sexual molestation in any report of genital bleeding from a child.

In the story Jesus met a Samaritan woman at Jacob's well in the heat of the day. Just as many modern incest victims are so full of shame they seem surprised that anyone speaks to them, the woman at the well was surprised that a Jewish man would speak to her, let alone condescend to drink from her vessel of water. When Jesus offered her living water, she inadvertently, perhaps sarcastically, alluded to the truth about Him in the question, "Are you greater than our father, Jacob, who gave us the well . . .?"

Jesus, in the drama, treated her with absolute seriousness in explaining the gift he had to offer. The woman grasped the offer initially as a possible escape from the toil of fetching water. She might have been an outcast of the society because of her sexual relationships and therefore required to draw water alone in the heat of the day rather than in the cool of the morning or evening with more respectable people in the community. If this were so, the offer of an alternative source of water that would permanently quench thirst would have been an escape from the degradation of her isolation as well.

The Samaritan woman, like many victims of sexual abuse in childhood, had more sexual partners than the number considered acceptable by the community. The Hebrew word for "husband" was also used as a name for a pagan deity, and the number of her husbands is analogous to the number of gods worshiped in Assyrian cults in Samaria. An authority figure in modern times who molests a child assumes god-like power over her, and sometimes uses religion to support his right to misuse her.

In any case, Jesus knew about all the men who had lorded over that woman at any stage of her life. She, who spoke the truth about Jesus in jest, probably before she was consciously aware of it, instantly comprehended the spiritual source of his prophetic perceptiveness. She asked him to settle the age-old dispute between Jews and Samaritans regarding proper worship. Jesus must have known that she, because she was a woman and probably an outcast in the community, could worship neither at the mountain shrine nor in the Temple in Jerusalem.

Perhaps she worshiped what she and her people could not know in the gentle breath of the Creator in the cool breeze of the evening. Perhaps she meditated alone under a fig tree, aware of the spirit of a God so awesome that His name could not be spoken. Perhaps Jesus recognized her from her private worship as he recognized Nathaniel. He reached across the chasm of taboo to include even such a woman into the community of those who worship rightly. He answered the ultimate question of authority for modern victims of abuse for whom even Christianity has been perverted. "The hour is coming and now is, when those who worship the Father worship Him in spirit and in truth, for such the Father seeks to worship Him."

NOTES

1. "Basic Facts about Sexual Child Abuse." A pamphlet published by The National Committee for Prevention of Child Abuse, Suite 510, 111 E. Wacker Drive, Chicago, Illinois 60601.

2. Information provided at a workshop entitled "Child Sexual Abuse and Its Relationship to Substance Abuse" sponsored by The National Council on Alcoholism, Michigan Division, 2875 Northwind Drive, Suite 225, East Lansing, Michigan 48823. September 30, 1982.

3. "Basic Facts About Sexual Child Abuse."

4. Workshop, "Child Sexual Abuse and Its Relationship to Substance Abuse."

5. Liepman, Michael R. "Some Theoretical Connections Between Family Violence and Substance Abuse." *The Catalyst* Vol. I, No. 3. An in-house publication of The National Council on Alcoholism, Michigan Division, 435 S. Washington Ave., Lansing, Michigan 48933.

6. Dietz, Christine A. and Craft, John L. "Family Dynamics of Incest: A New Perspective." *Social Casework. The Journal of Contemporary Social Work.* Family Service Association of America. 1980.

⟿ | *Chapter Seven*

Evangelism

I can't count the number of times it happened that one of the girls burst into my office and announced, "Guess what! I've been saved! And I gave up drugs, sex, and alcohol!"

Naturally I was delighted when any of them were touched by the divine in any fashion, and would never disparge such a confession. It couldn't hurt them to give up drugs, sex, and alcohol even for a few days. But I always wondered why they didn't give up lying, stealing, and fighting. Why did salvation mean, first and foremost, giving up anything? Does the Christian life consist only of being good until Jesus comes? What if He didn't come within the next week and a half and they got tired of waiting? Most of all I wondered why, just once, somebody didn't burst into my office and announce, "Guess what! I've been saved! And I love God with all my heart and soul and strength and I don't hate the guy who lives across the hall from me so much any more either."

Evangelism was the highest-priority goal of Kalamazoo Youth Ministry from its beginning. We all agreed that doing it was imperative. We agreed that evangelism is sharing the good news of salvation in both word and deed. The outcome we aimed for was faith. In serving people we gave substance to things hoped for; in our verbal witness, evidence of things unseen. There was no disagreement with that. And yet the very mention of the word evangelism aroused more spiritual anguish and emotional conflict among the staff than any other word. The trouble was that for each of us the word carried a heavy load of intensely personal emotional freight from each separate personal experience. That emotional freight was linked much more closely to the circumstances, style, and methods involved in individual religious experiences than it was to our beliefs about salvation as somewhat more mature Christians. Some of us met Jesus in highly charged revival meetings; others in a garden alone or in the intimate company of a close friend; and still others in the quiet dignity of a conventional church setting. The conflict over evangelism was not over the goal toward which we were headed, but over which train was bound for glory when the engines were all different colors!

Given the strength of our individual opinions and the diversity of our experiences, it was probably fortunate that most of us held the view that evangelism was a very personal and individual affair. This view, though problematic in itself, permitted a degree of freedom for each of us to practice and develop our own approaches until we could resolve some of our differences. I hid behind this shield of individuality more assiduously than the rest of the staff. The reason for this was that when as an adult I fell in love with scholarly theology, I had rejected the hellfire-and-brimstone style of evangelism I had witnessed as a child. My new love, however, was slow to provide me with an alternative approach. I was essentially isolated from any credible authority who could tell me how to do it, and instead tried to figure it out as if it were the day after the Fall of Man. My main problem with seeing evangelism or conversion primarily as a transaction between an individual and the Divine was the questionable role of another person in it. I was so afraid of interfering with that transaction, of messing it up somehow, that I hesitated to intervene at all. I could see myself as an agent of mercy. I saw only Christ as an agent of change. I had my hands full just persuading people to follow a few simple rules at The Next Door. How could I persuade them to undergo the radical spiritual transformation of rebirth?

I began to think of the role of evangelist as that of a midwife. The conception of the new person was from above, and the timing was in God's hands. The natural earthly self bore the travail. The natural self and the newborn Christian self needed assistance and nurturing in the beginning until they were integrated and able to function in some form of Christian community. The remarkable fact was that so many people were reborn and thrived like natural babies, whether they were welcomed into life by uneducated midwives, turned upside down and spanked into life in modern obstetrical settings, or placed lovingly on the mother's abdomen until breath came of its own accord and then given a warm, gentle bath.

Even with this reassurance I was about as terrified of the idea of presiding over a spiritual rebirth as I'd have been of assisting the delivery of a baby without expert help. Very little in the way of expert help was available to me. Literature that amounted to more than sales tactics was hard to come by. Most theologians I knew, if they weren't too embarrassed to discuss rebirth at all, were too abstract and academic about the process to be very helpful. We at the ministry were but ignorant midwives whose primary credentials consisted of having been reborn in some sense, and having survived the process. I didn't like the feeling of not knowing what I was doing in something so important, so I hung back from the enterprise of evangelism for the first two years. To continue with the birth metaphor, I provided comfort and nutrition in the way I treated prospective converts, and mopped up conflicts and cared for new Christians after the crucial phase was over.

Though I resisted the urgency of the threat of eternal damnation implicit in conventional evangelism, I was impressed with the high death rate of our guests. So many of them engaged in activities that sent their lives into dangerous downward spirals that I could no longer sit by and make no attempt to reach them at a spiritual level.

After two years of watching, thinking, reading and reflecting, I finally summoned the nerve to experiment with an overt intervention. It seemed the safe and helpful thing to do, when someone was suffering either physical or emotional pain, to teach systematic relaxation and meditation. I had never heard of anyone using meditation as an evangelistic technique before. I reasoned that since God is everywhere present, the young women could be taught to bring themselves into that presence, that is, to pray. I had been unsuccessful in invoking that presence for them by praying with them either silently or aloud. When I invited them to pray with me, they occasionally recited a few awkward phrases that didn't mean very much to them but which they thought I expected. Meditation, I thought, would slow them down so the awareness of God's presence could catch up with them and quiet their minds so they could hear His voice.

Most of my co-workers were horrified. For them, this was a powerful engine of the wrong color. I had learned meditation techniques while hooked up to a brainwave biofeedback machine for the purely secular purposes of increasing creativity and good feelings and decreasing blood pressure level and heartbeat rates. Worse still, in the minds of some, meditation was associated with hypnotism or with alien religions. What if going into a trance made people go crazy? What if they became Buddhists?

In answer to the first question, I was careful in my instructions not to assume the authority and control of a hypnotist, but to teach the subjects to induce a quiet, peaceful, relaxed state of mind within themselves. One definition of meditation was ordered thought. Ordered thought was a distinct improvement over the disordered thought most of them habitually engaged in. The light trances they were able to achieve were calming, and reduced the probability of psychotic manifestations. Although they didn't have profound religious experiences, it made them feel better.

As to the question of leading people away from Christianity, I didn't see how that could happen if I always carefully explained and instructed in Christian terms. I had learned from reading books by Thomas Merton, Henri Nouwen, and Anthony Bloom that meditation is very much a part of the Christian tradition. The chances of people turning away from Christianity were more likely increased if we waited for them to learn to meditate in non-Christian settings where other interpretations of the experience were taught.

The objections of the rest of the staff worried me enough, though, that I deemed it necessary to find or create some criteria for any plan of evangelism against which to test its theological soundness. Unable to find such criteria in the literature that was available to me at the time, I thought up an initial set which were based on the kind of outcome I wanted. They applied as much to the character of the evangelist as to the method or message to be used.

First and foremost, I wanted the young women to love God with heart, mind, and strength. I wasn't interested in turning them into copies of myself or in persuading them to adopt my ideas. Though I hoped that they would eventually find themselves in a Christian community or fellowship, the primary objective was not to get them to attend church. The approach had to be theocentric, God-centered. Evangelism happens by the grace of God and isn't dependent upon the method or character of the evangelist. But if I wanted to help it along, my first task was to become more God-centered. That required me to pray and study the Bible more.

Secondly, I wanted them to learn to love others as they loved themselves. This is the primary ethical component for both the convert and the evangelist. I was willing to leave the abstinence from drugs, sex, and alcohol for a later stage of development as a Christian. Whether the ethical component is love or puritanism, to put it first is to put the cart before the horse. The good news is not that if you become good you can be saved, but that through God's forgiving love you are not prevented by your guilt from becoming good. Though repentence is a desired outcome of conversion, it ought not to be seen so much as a onetime event, but as an ongoing process. The emphasis of repentence ought to be upon that ideal toward which one turns rather than the negative from which one turns away.

If love is the primary ethical component, then the evangelist simply must love people to start with, regardless of the apparent state of their souls. Our guests wouldn't listen to anything I said about anything else if they weren't convinced that I loved them. Without that they surely wouldn't listen to anything I said about God.

Third, I wanted my approach to be biblical. That could mean many different things to different people. For me it did not mean that everything I said was quoted from the Bible, nor that I used the Bible to prove what I was trying to say. To try to persuade someone that God is real because the Bible says so, and that the Bible is true because it is God's Word, is circular logic anyone could easily dismantle. For me, a biblical approach was one that pointed toward major themes and the most central ideals in the Bible. The central event is the crucifixion, of course. That was common knowledge even among the girls. I needed more than that story to illuminate its meaning. I appreciated the way Gabriel Fackre went about this in *The Christian Story*.[1] His approach, however, was directed toward a more literate audience than mine. I needed to condense biblical themes even more.

By this time, the rest of the staff was contemplating seriously the discipleship of their new converts. Without any disagreement, even from me, they selected a modern translation of the Heidelburg Catechism as a basic format for teaching new Christians what they needed to know. No one was dogmatic about the answers to the catechetical questions. We agreed quickly that the content of the Catechism, the Ten Commandments, the Lord's Prayer, and the Apostle's Creed comprised a survival kit that could serve as a guide throughout one's life in a variety of Christian settings. At last I found myself on common ground with the rest of the staff. No longer did I need to see evangelism as a solitary personal effort.

This common ground of agreement on the basics constituted

a firmer foundation for Christian community than if we had been blessed with the happy coincidence of liking each other and agreeing on all the peripheral issues at the outset. This foundation was anchored to a strong commitment in each of us that made us willing to be fools for the Good News, willing to make personal sacrifices and subject ourselves to physical danger in order to proclaim it. And further, this foundation was mortared together by our dependence on the structure of the ministry for the opportunity to live and proclaim the Good News and by our interdependence on each other for conviviality and physical protection.

Turning our individualistic swords into plowshares, our ideological spears into pruning hooks, was primarily a turning of intentionality. We possessed very efficient psychological mechanisms for holding grudges. Those mechanisms that had been used to divide us could be used to bind us together. A grudge is built by focusing attention on areas of disagreement, articulating differences, noticing little acts that touch us in sensitive areas and make us angry, and finally gossiping about those disagreements and resentments so that any semblance of cohesiveness is destroyed. This tool was just as efficient for building community as for destroying it. One needed only to look for areas of agreement, to articulate similarities while ignoring differences rather than vice versa. Each of us, no matter how dogmatic and argumentative, performed acts of mercy and kindness that touched others on the staff at a feeling level. Noticing those acts and appreciating them is a matter of intent. Gossiping about each other's good deeds served to build arches over the foundation. The gossip invariably found its way back to the perpetrator, which meant that goodness was supported by all the living stones through which the story had been carried. By supporting each other's good works and upholding each other's grasp of the truth, we formed arches through which God's light could shine and illuminate what we were doing. When we attempted to illuminate ourselves by explaining our points of view and talking about the things we had done, we weakened ourselves with pride and self-righteousness.

A Christian way of treating each other is to forgive each other's sin and weakness, not to return evil for evil, but to hold on to what is good. However irregular and haphazardly planned the temple of our ministry may have been, it became a sturdy, usable structure in which the reality of God's presence and grace was experienced by builders and guests alike.

The Lord's Prayer and the Ten Commandments comprised two pillars to which the biblical themes I found most meaningful could be attached, namely the Exodus story and the Sermon on the Mount. They comprised the backbone of my own spiritual life and were among the few portions of Scripture I had studied thoroughly enough to feel confident to expound.

The Exodus story and the Lord's Prayer pointed me toward a fourth criterion for a plan of evangelism. The image of the journey toward the Land of Promise and the prayer for the coming of the Kingdom strongly reflect the unique orientation of the Judeo-Christian tradition in the future. An evangelistic approach, therefore, should be open-ended, should move both the convert and the evangelist toward future growth and development as Christians. I could not assume the stance of one who had already arrived as a perfect Christian, as one who knew all the answers. The girls would have seen the artificiality of that in a minute. Instead, I engaged in an action and reflection process I later came to understand as praxis. I spoke and acted the best way I knew how in the midst of situations. Then I thought and reflected on what I had said and done and discussed it with anyone who would listen. This changed what I did in new situations. I was on a journey.

It was clear from our experience in ministry that our guests could not continue to grow and develop without the supporting and teaching of the Christian community. Left alone, they reverted to their old ways of thinking and behaving, as if Christianity were a disease from which they recovered, having suffered a mild case that left them resistant to future infection. If the germs we helped to implant in their lives were to thrive and grow, they needed infectious contact with a church or Christian fellowship. The youth ministry was simply unable to provide sustained inspiration and guidance throughout a person's life-time. Ours was primarily an entry-level operation.

Since the ministry was interdenominational and supported by a wide spectrum of the Christian community, we had a wide choice of groups to which we could send people. If a guest had a background in the Catholic Church, I nearly always tried to refer her to a local priest. If a Pentecostal or charismatic style had been part of her past, I could direct her to that kind of church.

Not all churches, however, were willing or able to accommodate the needs of multiple-problem converts. Much as I love my church, it wasn't suited to them. The idioms and concerns of a middle-class congregation did not address their needs. Part of my reluctance in inviting them to my church was selfish. I didn't like the idea of driving all over town on Sunday morning to transport them there, and I needed time to worship when I did not have to attend personally to their needs of the moment. Sharon and Nico's church was able to make them feel much more comfortable and easily took their idiosyncrasies in stride. They routinely loaded their station wagon full of people who lived or gathered at The Next Door. They, like me, expressed the need for time apart from taking care of people to worship.

Although I avoided arguments over which church a new convert ought to attend, I had some additional ideas about ongoing growth that caused plenty of arguments. Since I saw conversion more as a beginning than as an ending, I did not want to give the impression in my evangelism that Christianity would mean an end to all their problems. If they were persuaded initially by testimonies of answered prayers, miraculous solutions to problems, healing of illness, they found their faith shaken the first time they didn't get exactly what they prayed for. Better to present a picture of Christ as one who is with us in adversity than as one who makes life painless. Converts who were persuaded by the typical revivalist approach seemed to have little idea of what to do after rebirth except perhaps to invite others to similar meetings or to re-enact their own conversion by passing it on like a chain letter. It may have been easier to pass out tracts on a street corner than to learn to love their enemies, but hardly conducive to the kind of growth I had in mind.

Converts who had been taught a very literal interpretation of the Bible required the equivalent of another conversion experience to cope with the fact that the Bible contains some discrepancies in its witness and some material that is fictional and symbolic. Circumventing this problem was easier than it might appear at first glance. The culture is steeped in television, movies, and rock music. Even our guests realized that stories and poems don't have to be absolutely factual to be meaningful and true. If, like Fackre, we told stories as stories, as interpretations of experience, then the prospective convert could be invited to make God's story his or her own story, and to interpret life in that way. Then, when we got around to talking about Jonah, we could discuss the persistence of God's call rather than the marine life of the Mediterranean.

Even though I tried not to be dogmatic and polemical about these opinions, the controversies they provoked were extremely painful. There were those on the staff who thought that I was discounting the prayers which proved their faith, and that the reason I saw so many unanswered prayers was my lack of faith. There were those who believed that the primary and highest calling of a Christian is to pass on the Good News, and that I was doing my job poorly because I was less vigorous about it than they. There were those who believed that I was a heretic, and accused me of not believing in the Bible at all if I didn't take the King James Version to be literally factual. These conflicts with other Christians hurt far more than conflicts with those who made no claim to faith. We held in common, however, a serious calling to care for our guests and an agreement about central portions of the Scripture. This commonality kept us together and sustained us through many agonizing conflicts. When I could see past the pain, I was able to learn from others' approaches and to identify characteristics which contributed to their appeal. These characteristics reflected my pragmatic concern that my method be appropriate to the situation.

First of all, I noticed that most approaches that appealed successfully to people made very specific applications of the message to present-day life experiences. Whether the application was ethical opposition to drugs, sex, and alcohol or interpretation of current events according to the imagery in the book of Revelation, it was closely tied to things that could be seen, heard, or touched in everyday life. My role as a counselor put me in touch with very intimate, sensitive, and important material in the lives of my young women. Listening carefully enough to understand their stories accurately made possible any number of specific interpretive applications of the basic message I had in mind.

Secondly, successful approaches reached people at a feeling level. Some methods generated a high level of emotional intensity. Since the girls' emotions tended to run high anyway, I had no need to stir them up. Listening carefully to their feelings as well as to the content of their stories helped me to aim my comments and interpretations to touch their emotions.

Third, successful approaches employed easily understandable language and emphasized one or two uncomplicated ideas. At The Next Door anything I said had to be simple enough to be said in about five minutes and understood by people with a third grade education. Because of the stressful nature of the girls' lives, this was the approximate level of new learning they could accommodate and the average length of their attention spans. This wasn't easy for someone like me who thinks in paragraphs and chapters.

Fourth, an appropriate method had to be earnest and sincere. It would have been artificial for me to have used any high pressure tactics. The young women were highly suspicious generally, and could sense the slightest whiff of artificiality two rooms away. My low-key approach alleviated their suspicions to a degree, and was more consistent with my personal style and taste.

Because my ideas about evangelism were so different from those of most of the other people on the staff, because my theological education was limited, and because I was isolated from other people who could or would discuss such ideas with me, I was constantly haunted with the worry that I was going about it all wrong. I longed and searched for a widely accepted test for the soundness of any improvised model. My own church explained its mission as a fourfold witness: *leitourgia, koinonia, kerygma,* and *diakonia*—worship, community, proclamation, and service. This was not an end in itself, but rather a four-sided pillar of fire on the horizon which we follow for the sake of where it leads us, toward shalom.

It was only after I had left the youth ministry and begun to write that I realized that the unity and completeness of that fourfold witness of evangelism provided the ideal theological standard for a system of evangelism. The model was cited in *Human Liberation in a Feminist Perspective—A Theology* by Letty Russell,[2] from whom I was taking a class at Princeton Theological Seminary. When this dimension of its usefulness dawned on me, I thought it was so elegantly classic it must have been thought of by somebody like St. Athanasius in the fourth century! To my delighted surprise I found the work cited to be that of Hans Hoekendijk, Letty Russell's husband. He wrote:

> This is how it started. In September, 1949, I had, with fear and trembling, to "perform" for the first time as the Secretary of Evangelism of the World Council of Churches. . . .
>
> Well, CIMADE, (a French youth group committed to functionalizing the historia Jesu among prisoners of war and refugees) had a very precise demand: "Give us; in the shortest possible shorthand, the biblical key concepts to understand what we have been doing and, far more importantly, what we are supposed to do." Unable to make the shorthand even shorter, I came up with four such concepts: kerygma, koinonia, diakonia, and leitourgia. . . .

. . . .What was intended to be an ad hoc description of one particular evangelistic enterprise entered literature as a normative model for all experiments in communicating the gospel. I agree, as long as we are aware that this is a possible configuration of the dimensions of evangelism and one that may be of some help in devising a typology of the various styles of communicating the gospel. We witness that single dimensions of the total act of evange-lism are abstracted from the whole and absolutized. With only a little imaginative effort we can count off all present ventures as either one-sidedly and not seldom, fanatically kerygma-centered, or koinonia-oriented, or diakon-ia-focused.

The intention, of course was to keep the dimensions together and inter-related. According to situational needs, we might feel compelled to emphasize one particular as-pect, without ever neglecting the others. . . .

By looking separately at these . . . [four] dimensions of gospel communication we always run the risk of either isolating or over-emphasizing one aspect of a total event. . . . We have convinced verbalists who only know of a word-event next to the activists who plead for a moratorium on all proclamation . . . I would like to suggest, however, that in all communication of the gospel, kerygma, diakonia, [leitourgia] and koinonia are inextricably bound togeth-er. . . .

The historia Jesu has to be told, shared in service, and expressed in corporate commitment [and worship], so that it will be communicated and ever more people will live within the horizons of hope: life, righteousness, and thus, God's will done on earth.[3]

What is one to do with these lists of criteria? Improvise! Improvisation is not saying any old thing one feels like saying, or inventing an approach on the spot as one goes along. Im-provisation is a musical term that describes how jazz musicians play together. They are skilled with their instruments and un-derstand music both theoretically and subjectively. They have basic themes and chord sequences that are agreed upon and rehearsed. They synchronize their rhythm, listen carefully to each other, and adapt and flow with their respective melodies. Good musicians don't interrupt or upstage each other. They give themselves to the music and to each other and create experiences that express feeling differently each time they are played. Just so, the evangelist must be skilled in playing the instrument of him- or herself in life, be sensitive to the rhythm of God's movement, and listen carefully to others. With love and with great respect for others, the evangelist sustains the chord of leitourgia, koinonia, kerygma, and diakonia as background for the melodies of shared life stories. When the time is right for a solo, the familiar theme of the biblical story can be played. All the while, the movement is from dissonance to harmony, from alienation to shalom.

One afternoon I was sitting in my office about a week and a half after one of those spectacular conversions away from drugs, sex and alcohol. The young convert appeared in my office, ashamed and heartbroken. Temptation had overcome her in the form of a newly met young man who had taken her to a party with drugs. One thing led to another until all the fine resolutions she'd made were broken. "I don't think," she confided tearfully, "that I was really saved at all."

"Oh, my dear lamb," I said, almost in tears myself, "of course you were saved! Don't ever doubt that or forget it for a minute! Jesus loves you just as much right this minute as he did when you gave your heart to him last week. And he knew even then that this would happen. Being saved doesn't mean that you never sin again. It means that your sins can't bind you or hold you back any more because you know that you can be forgiven."

"But I thought that when I was baptized that all my sins were washed away, and that was the end of my old life."

"In a way that's true, in the sense that your old life no longer has the power to trap you. You know that you were like a slave in the family you were born into, and forced to do things that were bad and terribly bad for you. Do you know the story in Exodus about how God went about freeing the slaves?"

"Sort of. I remember a little about it from Sunday School."

"You remember that the people God had chosen were slaves in Egypt, making bricks and building pyramids. Moses came along and there were all the plagues and everything until after the last plague when all the firstborn children in Egypt died. And then all the slaves took off into the desert and the Pharoah's army took after them. They got as far as the Red Sea, and the army was closing in behind them, so there they were just like you before you were baptized, between the Devil and the deep blue sea."

"I remember talking to you about being between the Devil and the deep blue sea."

"Do you remember what happened next in Exodus?"

"Sure. It was in the movie, *The Ten Commandments*. Charlton Heston held up his hands and God parted the waters, and the slaves got across and the waters went back together again and drowned all the Egyptians."

"Right. And that's like what happened to you when you were baptized."

"I don't get it."

"Well, when you went forward in that service, there was no way out for you. When you went down into that baptismal tank, you were a slave, running for your life. When you came out on the other side, you were no longer a slave. You were a free person and you gave your life to the God who saved you."

"What went wrong?"

"The same thing that went wrong for the people of Israel. They thought they were going to trek off and find the land of milk and honey after three days. Instead, they found themselves wandering in the desert without any water. They said to Moses, 'Hey man, this is a ripoff! Let's go back to Egypt. At least there we had food to eat.' Didn't you start missing the things you used to do, and feel like being a Christian was a ripoff?"

"Yeah. I couldn't have any fun!"

"Well, the Israelites did the same thing you did. They built a golden calf and had a high old time. It took forty years of wandering around in the wilderness to learn how to live and get their needs met a different way."

"Are you trying to tell me that it's going to take forty years to learn how to be a Christian?"

"It'll take the rest of your life! You don't think I've got it down pat, do you?"

"I thought you did."

"Well, I don't. You've been around here enough and watched me enough to know that every day in this office I mess up in ways that are just as damaging as what you did last night. Remember that day you were screaming at me that I didn't have it all together, and you were right."

She laughed, "Yeah."

"Okay. Well, we've still got that old slave mentality. You still feel the need to take drugs and drink to escape from pain and despair. You still feel guilty if you say no to a man because that's the way you survived as a slave."

"How am I going to get over that?"

"I don't know if any of us ever will completely. The thing we have to do is just not to get lost in the wilderness. We've got to keep chasing after that pillar of fire on the horizon, and give each other a loud whistle when we start going off in the wrong direction. It seems like we're not getting anywhere because the sand dunes all look alike, day after day. But every once in a while, we come to a mountain and we can look back and see how far we've come. And every once in a while we get little glimpses of what it's really like to be free and what it feels like to be in God's kingdom. And we tell those things to each other, too, to keep us going."

"So here we are in the wilderness, right? Side by side."

"You got it. Want a hug?"

NOTES

1. Fackre, Gabriel. *The Christian Story: A Narrative Interpretation of Basic Christian Doctrine.* Grand Rapids, Michigan: William B. Eerdmans Publishing Company, 1978.

2. Russell, Letty M. *Human Liberation in a Feminist Perspective—A Theology.* Philadelphia, Pennsylvania: The Westminster Press, 1974.

3. Hoekendijk, Hans. *Horizons of Hope.* Nashville, Tennessee: Tidings Press, 1970.

✴ | *Chapter Eight*

Burnout

Anyone who contemplates an intensive ministry of service should know about burnout. People who knew of Kalamazoo Youth Ministry and friends of the staff often expressed their concern for us. We were frequently asked, "How do you stand to work in a place like that day after day? Don't you get depressed?" None of us wished to complain; yet the truth was that we all felt frustrated and discouraged at least some of the time. We could not expect to work with people who were depressed and miserable, who remained depressed and miserable despite our best efforts, without experiencing some of those feelings ourselves. We expected not to feel good all the time, and generally accepted the burden of feeling sad, fearful, and sometimes even angry. These feelings in themselves were not necessarily destructive, and we recovered quickly. When our emotions were aroused with such frequency and intensity that we did not have enough time and energy to recover, we became drained, frustrated, and resentful. When our recuperative powers themselves were diminished, our motivation was threatened. Then we faced the crisis of inspiration, of hope, and perhaps even of faith, that the term burnout connotes.

Burnout, to some degree, occured in all of us who worked at

the ministry fulltime. It followed a regular pattern. We experienced long periods of hard work during which we saw little progress. We became frustrated, exhausted, and perhaps even ill. Fighting for control, we resisted the inclination to take life easy and rest, and forced ourselves to work harder still. As we wrestled with our internal motivation, we expended energy at an increased level. We had less of it, therefore, to invest in relationships with family and friends who might have nurtured us. As those relationships deteriorated, the draining of our emotions accelerated. All of our vulnerabilities were exposed. Our resistance was lowered to the contagious diseases to which we were constantly exposed. We came down with colds and flu which seemed to hang on and on. Any vices to which we were inclined became serious temptations. None of us was immune to the temptation to misuse his or her body. Some of us ate too much, others smoked heavily, and a few reverted to alcohol, drugs, or illicit sex. Those who engaged in the more destructive of those activities had previous histories of doing so. Some vices were less detrimental than others to the ministry as a whole, and less damaging to an individual's self-control and ability to recover. The misuses that were publicly embarrassing to the ministry tended to be more tragic than those that were socially acceptable, because reconciliation was more difficult. When people resigned in disgrace or had to be fired, guilt and shame divided them from the Christian community, sometimes permanently. Those who ate too much, smoked, or who directed frustration and resentment against other people were no less guilty, but the judgement was less severe and the external pressure to leave the ministry less urgent.

Frustration, more than mere unpleasantness, contributed to burnout in our experience. Frustration is a personal response, born of dissatisfaction, bathed in resistance and resentment, nurtured by a perception of powerlessness and helplessness. The satisfaction we most desired, and that which we were most powerless to effect, was improvement in the lives of those we served. Many of the guests at The Doors functioned at very low levels in daily life, and required a great deal of prompting just to take care of their belongings and to exist in the environment without causing trouble. With many of them we invested huge amounts of time and energy before they were able to make the first steps toward improvement of their lives. The progress that we saw was minimal and painfully slow. Some of them never made any significant changes, and kept returning to us with the same problems over and over again. Even more discouraging was to see their problems passed on to another generation. We were among the first to learn when one of them was pregnant and were expected to provide help and support during a pregnancy and after the baby was born. In order to be effective we had to love and hope the best for the new parents and babies alike. When we saw the parents treat their children as they themselves had been treated, we felt our love and hope assaulted, our sensitivities enraged, and ourselves utterly helpless to effect any meaningful change.

A second source of frustration was the environment of the ministry itself. The house was often cluttered and dirty, and smelled of people who did not bathe or launder clothing frequently enough. Household appliances, wiring, plumbing failed constantly. Often we were too busy or too tired to clean, and did not have enough time or money to make needed repairs. The houses always had cockroaches. No matter how often the exterminators serviced the houses, we could accomplish little more than to sustain the problem at a tolerable level. Noise was a constant annoyance, especially in the summertime. We could ask people to be quiet and turn down the television set inside the house; but when the windows were open, loud arguments and rock music could be heard all over the neighborhood. Sometimes noisy parties lasted all night, and there was little we or the police could do about them. The houseparents at The Next Door and the resident counselors at The Open Door experienced many nights of disrupted sleep.

Staff members who were economically dependent upon the ministry were frustrated by its financial difficulties. Our salaries were low to begin with, and paychecks arrived late approximately half the time. Most could not regularly afford little luxuries such as meals in restaurants and nice clothing. Recreational activities were limited by cost. Vacations had to be economical, and were sometimes disrupted by malfunctioning automobiles and the failures of poor equipment for camping.

The houseparents and I experienced some frustration in feeling that we were never really off duty. Because the Seinens lived at The Next Door, they could not help hearing disturbances which occured during their free time. Even though other staff was available, they always wondered if their help was needed. Events that took place at The Open Door concerned their lives directly because their windows looked out on the parking lot which people traversed to and from The Open Door. Sometimes their windows were even broken. They kept food and household supplies in their apartment and in the basement, and their time alone together as a family was frequently interrupted by a knock at their door by staff from either house who needed something. Some visitors would knock at their door just wanting to chat with them, not realizing that a social call on their part might feel like work to the Seinens.

I did not wish to be completely separated from The Next Door when I went home. I thought about problems and looked for solutions when I was off duty.

I worried about having enough volunteers to permit the Seinens and me adequate respite, and sometimes worked on recruiting and scheduling volunteers in the evening at home. The Next Door was like a beloved child with many problems; I could never fully forget about it.

If the volunteers or the houseparents were having a problem with which I could help, I preferred to be called on the telephone. I found it easier to deal with crises as they came up than to try to make sense of them when I returned in the morning. I worried less when I was assured that I could be called upon if needed. The girls called me at home sometimes, too. I did not encourage this, but I did not have an unlisted number.

I had considerably more control over my privacy than the Seinens, but my sense of responsibility was almost as constant. My greatest frustration with the constancy of demands was being unable to take time off for illness. I did not want to overburden the Seinens, and volunteers were not always available on short notice. Therefore, I often worked while I was sick, and felt very sorry for myself when I did.

My problems coordinating my personal life with the ministry were different from those of the houseparents. The values, concerns, and expectations of the ministry differed drastically from those of my family, friends, and church. In the suburbs I was expected to acquire, maintain, and preserve possessions and assets; in my work environment, the purpose of resources was to give them away. During the day I concerned myself with issues of survival; in the evenings my primary concerns were for comfort, convenience, security, and luxury. My best expectation of a working day was to endure it with acceptance and grace. Those who surrounded me in private life were oriented to success and achievement. My family, though tolerant and accepting, was not in full sympathy with the causes for which I labored or my daily problems, nor was I fully sympathetic with theirs. Yet I was sufficiently involved and attuned to middle-class values to feel slightly hypocritical among those with whom I worked, who lived in poverty. In most social gatherings I felt uneasy, uncomfortable, and lonely, and was rarely able to relax and have fun. I had to make special efforts to cultivate and maintain a few close friendships with people who understood both of my realities. I was very grateful for my volunteers and a few other patient souls who prevented my complete isolation.

Everyone on the youth ministry staff experienced the frustration of having to shift personal feelings to the background in order to attend fully to the work. All of us felt intense emotions about our personal interactions with people both off duty and on. These emotions did not always dissipate quickly even after a night's sleep.

Though the more or less constant threat of danger was a

stress factor, we generally handled fear better than anger. As I mentioned in an earlier chapter, theft, vandalism, and assaults were common occurrences in the neighborhood. Most of the people who were really violent knew us, and would not have hurt us. Yet there were occasional personality conflicts, and a few who were so psychotic we never knew quite what to expect from them. Some danger was involved when we had to confront people who were creating disturbances. Generally we feared more for each other than for ourselves. Sharon and I worried about Nico when he went out to break up a fight. Nico felt protective of all the women on the premises, incuding Sharon, the volunteers, and me.

Some events were frightening without being particularly dangerous. The Seinens awakened one night to find an inebriated man sitting at the foot of their bed. Nico calmly ushered him out of the house, but we never did figure out how he got in. When the Seinens' sons were babies, the attentions of some of the residents were disconcerting. From time to time, young women came to us following the loss of a child through death, voluntary adoption, or removal by the court. A chill went down Sharon's back when one of these said, "Oh, your baby is so cute, I think I'll kidnap him and take him with me!" None ever tried, but those were the kinds of fears of which our nightmares were made.

Anger was a greater problem because, as good Christians, we were reluctant to express it. Conflict among staff sapped our energy and enthusiasm more quickly than anger directed toward the guests. Each of us had strong convictions about how the ministry ought to operate. Each of us needed cooperation and consideration from other staff members to put ideas into action, and to make life bearable. When we did not live up to each other's expectations, we felt angry. When we tried to effect changes in daily operations and did not receive the necessary cooperation, we felt extremely frustrated. Widely varied approaches to Christianity and differences in semantics and ideology set up barriers among us. When we were overworked, pressed for time, and frustrated, we were not always consistent and prompt in following through with decisions even when we agreed on them. When conflicts arose we were often reluctant to confront each other, and were sometimes defensive about criticism.

The experience that stood above all others as the greatest single frustration for every member of the staff was the perception of not being heard and taken seriously. When we felt unable to make ourselves understood or felt that our ideas, feelings and wishes were not accorded the importance they deserved, we became frightened, angry, and distrustful. Poor communication compounded resentment. Cliques and factions arose, and we isolated ourselves from each other. Unresolved conflict among the staff was costlier than any other frustration to our inspiration and hopes for the ministry.

Some of the aforementioned frustrations could be dealt with before they grew into crises. Other circumstances were not within our power to change and we had to find ways of thinking about them which helped us to accept and endure them.

Our power to effect lasting differences in the lives of those we served was limited indeed. We learned to look for small, temporary differences over which we had some control. We could effect the difference between shelter and homelessness at any given time, and the difference between hunger and adequate nutrition while people remained with us. For some this was all we could do. The guests who made the most productive use of our services were those who stayed for short periods of time, resolved their immediate crises, and went on with their lives independent of us. We never heard from them again. Instead of worrying about our lambs after they left our fold, we assumed that they would return if they needed our services again. If we heard nothing about them, we trusted that they were safe in God's care, and prayed for miracles.

Some of our guests were unpleasant to live with and difficult to relate to. We tried to view our problems with them not as annoyances, but as our purpose for being in ministry. If, after all, they were able to care for themselves and were easy to get along with, they would not have needed us.

We learned to evaluate ourselves on the basis of the quality of the service rendered rather than on the use that was made of our service. We learned to give ourselves credit for having treated people well and having made them feel better. We learned not to be destructive in our self-deprecation when we were unable to treat people as well as we might have wished.

Virtually any person or situation could be endured with love temporarily. We found it useful to remind ourselves that nothing was permanant. One moment, one hour, one day was manageable. To concentrate too much attention on either the past or the future made frustrations seem endless and unendurable. The Seinens were particularly skilled at thinking and living in the present tense. They simply served God moment by moment, neither remembering the sacrifices of the previous hour nor dreading what might be required of them in the next. This did not preclude our thinking and talking about past events in order to learn from them, nor from identifying patterns that were helpful in developing strategies for the future. We tried, rather, to avoid accumulating feelings about the past or indulging in feelings about the future over which we had no control.

The perception of ourselves as indispensible not only contributed to burnout, but was a form of pride. Rushing to the rescue at the first sign of disruption, when someone else was on duty, sometimes precipitated more crises than it alleviated. Replaying situations over and over in my mind when I should have been resting or attending to my family served no purpose at all. When I was worrying about situations over which I had no control, I asked myself "Am I playing God or am I serving God?" The ministry, after all, was His, as were the people who came there for help. The single most helpful piece of advice I would offer to someone working in this kind of ministry is to ask him or herself that question. We learned from simple necessity to trust God to watch over things we could do nothing about.

At the same time, we could not afford to spend our energy feeling tense, resentful, and frustrated about circumstances that were within our control. Household frustrations were the ones that yielded most predictably to personal effort. If I grew tired of my office looking like a distribution center for used clothing, the simplest way to remedy my frustration was to clean it out! Just as important was to learn not to view The Next Door as personal territory, and dirt and clutter as an invasion. My standards of neatness were generally lower than the Seinens'. I seemed to be able to shut my eyes to horrendous messes, and be oblivious to my environment when I was busy with people. Sometimes the Seinens cleaned my office as a special treat for me, and, I suspect, because they couldn't stand the clutter! When painting or repairs were needed and we could not raise funds or volunteer labor, we did what needed to be done at our own expense. That was more practical than feeling sorry for ourselves and resenting the organization's inefficiencies.

We learned to manage our economic resources efficiently. We did not need to spend a lot of money to have fun and to feel good about our lives. We dressed inexpensively, ate cheaply, and were not embarrassed about being unable to afford certain things. We lived below our economic means in order to save money for the seasons when paychecks were sparse. Most of us found it more difficult to overcome a feeling of guilt about spending money for our own pleasure and comfort than to live within our incomes. Both were necessary.

Planning carefully for vacations and providing adequate time off was a team effort on the part of the staff. We were more inclined to overwork than to complain about the excessive demands the situation made of us, and felt more comfortable insisting upon respite for each other than for ourselves. The reliability and the quality of our time off was more crucial than the frequency of respite. So that the Seinens were disturbed as little as possible during their time off, we made an effort to get supplies and conduct business with them during their working hours. I would not let guests knock at their door during their free time, if I could help it. They were so inclined to be helpful, I had to remind them occasionally not to jump to answer every

knock at their door and accommodate every request so cheerfully, so that my adamant attempts to ensure their privacy did not
appear foolish. The telephone system permitted them freedom
from hearing its ringing during the day, and I screened even
personal calls for them. When communication could not be
delayed until their working hours, I slipped notes under their
door, which was less obtrusive than knocking and talking with
them. They and the executive director provided backup assistance to volunteers, so that I was rarely disturbed at home on
my day off.

Longer periods of complete separation from the youth ministry refreshed us more than more frequent, shorter vacations.
The Seinens left for an entire month each summer. If we had
not been so fortunate as to find good people to move into their
apartment and provide supervision for residents during that
time, we would have closed the facility for a month rather than
ask them to sacrifice that time away. I was permitted two weeks
of vacation each year. In addition, I took, at my own expense,
an annual three-week study leave during which I took a summer
class at an eastern seminary. I thoroughly enjoyed a complete
change of environment apart even from my family, and could
think of no recreation I would have enjoyed more than to
immerse myself completely in theological study.

Our concern for each other was both pragmatic and genuine.
Even when I disagreed with the Seinens, I never felt that I could
find another couple as hardworking and dedicated to replace
them. If I were to keep them, I had to take good care of them.
For equally practical reasons, they extended themselves to accommodate my views and eccentricities, and were very tolerant
of me. Our decision to learn to love each other required conscious effort. Deliberately and conscientiously we created an
atmosphere in which the honest expression of opinions and
feelings was encouraged. In time we learned to trust each other
and came to feel deep mutual respect and affection. We believed
in each other's sincerity and goodness of intent. There was no
anger between us, no hidden suspicions of laziness, of sabotage,

no will to control each other. We knew that each of us was doing the best that he or she could. In the extreme tenderness that developed between us, the forgiveness and the extra efforts made on the other's behalf were not burdensome, but genuine acts of love.

We learned to be straightforward about our feelings and to identify and articulate our own needs. We were responsible for monitoring our own accumulations of unresolved feelings and for finding ways to take care of ourselves. When the loneliness of my fragmented life became unbearable and I needed more listening than my friends could afford, I experienced no shame in seeking the help of a professional counselor. A ministry that was better funded than ours would be wise to provide such an option for employees as a routine policy. In the absence of that fringe benefit, our guests constituted the best referral service imaginable. They sampled the work of virtually every therapist and counselor in the city, and reported unerringly which ones were helpful and which could be trusted! Anyone who could help them could easily help me; anyone who liked them and was patient with them would enjoy working with me and understand the difficulty of my situation. I was never disappointed when I trusted their judgment.

I also used a journal to monitor my feelings, to conduct therapy with myself, and to evaluate my work. I was often able to ventilate feelings and to let them go simply by writing them down. When I read what I wrote, I could see patterns in my thinking and develop strategies for altering them. Writing also kept me in touch with a sense of adventure in my work, with its pizzazz. When circumstances were at their worst, I could still enjoy them as good stories. By the end of four years I had written approximately fifteen hundred pages!

Through writing, useful formulas for managing both fear and anger evolved. In the simplest possible terms, fear is what a person feels when an adverse event is expected. To alleviate the feeling, I had first to identify what I was afraid of experiencing. As I explored my thoughts carefully, I often found that my fears revolved around fantasies that were unlikely ever to happen. If, after realizing the improbability of my expectations, I still felt scared, I systematically listed things I could do to reduce the probability even further, things I could do to reduce the severity of the event, and things I could do if my worst expectations came to pass. If I could not control events, I could at least control my reaction to them. After I acted on my preventative measures, I simply refused to allow my mind to dwell on unpleasant possibilities. Most of the events that I feared never happened, and it was a complete waste of time to suffer from catastrophies that existed only in my imagination. Even if they did happen, there was no point in suffering in advance of the actuality. With practice I learned to let the evil of the day be sufficient thereto. With experience I learned to trust God to enable us all to endure, perhaps in unforeseeable ways, as He had throughout the history of the ministry.

My strategy for resolving anger required more self-examination. When I was angry with another person for more than a brief period of time, I found that I was usually angry with myself for some reason. Most often I felt anger toward people whose faults or weaknesses were similar to mine. Throughout my life I had grown so accustomed to controlling my expressions of anger that I had repressed the awareness that I felt like doing the very act that made me angry. I so much wanted to see myself as a good person that I also clung to anger to avoid admitting guilt of my own. In my journal I wrote letters to people with whom I was angry, and then imagined myself as the other person, and answered my letters. Generally I found that when I was angry I did not need vindication as much as I needed forgiveness, not for the anger itself but for the guilt that lay behind it.

Some of the uncomfortable feelings and frustrations did not yield to easy resolution. These were the feelings that tempted some to seek relief in destructive ways. Certain spare time activities permitted escape from these feelings while enhancing rather than diminishing our self-control. Vigorous physical exercise was one of the healthiest ways to make ourselves feel better. It relieved muscle tension and at the same time provided an experience of power and control when we felt powerless and out of control. Nico suffered from an ongoing frustration with chaos and disorder around him, and found relief in working jigsaw puzzles and sorting his stamp collection. I was prone to periods of depression and sadness, and found comfort in knitting. The repetitive motions of my hands and the softness of the yarn had a calming effect on me. When I found myself entering one of those periods, and could do little or nothing about the situation or my attitude toward it, I undertook a needlework project of the approximate magnitude of the problem. Some problems were afghan-sized, others sweater-sized, and some were likely to be resolved in the time required to knit a muffler or a pair of mittens. Estimating the duration of my feelings reduced them to manageable proportions in my mind, and I invariably finished my grief before I finished the garment I was knitting.

Sharon and I engaged in a number of eccentric forms of play together. For six months or so we experimented with soybean recipes, an enterprise which was inexpensive, novel, and a little humorous. It also alleviated some of our feelings about the shortage of food in the world. At another point we undertook to teach ourselves Greek. I found that I could conjugate verbs in small periods of time when I might have been doodling. Though I never advanced beyond the sixth chapter in the textbook I borrowed, the attempt helped me to feel less frustrated with my limited ability to understand the New Testament. We both like to play with pens and paper, and took up calligraphy for a while. There was an ironic touch of humor in chore lists and memos requesting toilet paper lettered in chancellery italic script.

The most powerful antidote for burnout was prayer. Prayer kept alive our hopes for the people we worked with. Prayer helped us to see beyond the domestic and economic problems and rested us when there was no respite from work and confusion. In prayer we were not alone, but were heard, understood, forgiven and comforted at the core of our being. It enabled us to yield our frustration with situations over which we had no control to the One who was in ultimate control. Prayer was a way to be refilled when we were spent, inspired when we were desperate, and healed when we were sick in body and soul. With prayer we found ourselves on the other side of the chilly waters of burnout, not always sure how we had arrived, but profoundly grateful for our deliverance.

Despite all the remedies I was able to devise, I suffered a serious case of burnout in the spring of 1980. I had been the director of The Next Door less than two years.

For reasons I have never fully understood, I have always had a tendency to feel depressed in the springtime. The holidays that kept my spirit alive with anticipation and inspiration were behind me. My family, whose life revolved around the rhythms of the academic year, looked forward to the freedom of summer. The Next Door was usually busier in the summer than at any other time. The quiet, restful hours of winter darkness gave way to the incresed activity, noise, and demands of longer daylight. Heat, humidity, and invasion of insects made it less comfortable than in winter. While the rest of creation was bursting with new life, I felt my energy ebb as though I were bleeding to death.

All of the weakest points of my character became open wounds. I lacked the discipline to keep myself in good physical condition through proper exercise and diet. Exhausted by emotional turmoil and physical inactivity at work, I vegetated in front of the television set in the evenings. I developed chronic back pain. Craving anything that provided instant gratification, I munched and snacked on junk food. Gaining weight detracted from my self-image and inclined me to be even less active.

I also had a narcissistic need to be admired and appreciated and a tendency to depend upon the esteem of other people for my sense of self-worth. After nearly two years, the novelty of my job had worn thin and my friends no longer found it remarkable. The number of friends on whom I could rely to make me feel good about myself had dwindled. Some moved away or changed jobs; others became bored with me. I felt very lonely.

My energy and enthusiasm for both my job and my home life diminished, and the conflict between the two reached crisis proportions. I felt myself torn between the desire to work harder and harder to meet successfully the needs of The Next Door and the desire to retreat into suburban domestic life and be cared for. I was tired of spending my days with people who seemed never to change, and discouraged with my powerlessness to help them. Work bored me because it did not satisfy my need to feel successful, valued, and loved. Having difficulty facing each day of work, I resented the convenience, comfort, and security of my home which Marlin worked so hard to provide. I was experiencing a deep internal struggle, a schism at the core of my being. I grew increasingly detached both from my work and from my home life, and my isolation became virtually impenetrable. I had lost my motivation to do practically anything.

Marlin was facing the problem of living with someone who was depressed and miserable without himself becoming depressed and miserable. He was tired of having a wife who was constantly exhausted and preoccupied with the affairs of The Next Door. He was bored with my complaints about it, and unable to listen empathically. He reminded me frequently that if I didn't like my job, I could quit. I resented this because it denied the importance and validity of what I was doing. Both of us were heartbroken over the alienation between us.

I sought the help of an expensive psychologist who pressed me to do something about my situation rather than to reconcile myself to it. He confronted me vigorously with the alternatives of quitting my job and/or getting a divorce. Contemplating either alternative added grief to the despair I was already feeling.

I wept all the way to work every morning and all the way home every evening. I sat helplessly tearful through church services and prayer times. I did not like to burden my volunteers with my personal problems. Some of my friends feared the intensity of my desperation and no one wanted to listen to me.

When I wasn't weeping openly, I walked around numb with internal pain. Conversations swirled around me like music on a cheap radio which I could neither hear properly nor turn off. My body felt numb, as if I were an astronaut walking around in a space suit, insulated from feeling any external sensation.

The Seinens stayed by me as well as they could. They encouraged me to take time off, even though it meant their having to run The Next Door themselves while I was away. Since I was angry with practically everyone and no one could comfort me, I decided to go away by myself to fast and pray and to take long walks and give myself some exercise. The Seinens helped me to arrange the use of a cabin on a lake a few hours' drive north in Michigan. The cabin belonged to Barbie's parents, who were kind enough to let me use it free of charge.

I could have left on Friday, but I dragged my feet. I went shopping for books. Elizabeth O'Connor's books, *Search for Silence*[1] and *The Eighth Day of Creation*,[2] had been recommended to me. My search for the books led me to a Lutheran Conference held on the university campus, where I decided to stay and hear a couple of lectures in the afternoon and evening.

I still remember part of the evening lecture. It was delivered by a woman seminary president, but my journal does not record her name. The theme of the lecture was, "Jesus is Lord, and we are His. Lift up your hearts." I do not remember the articulate, systematic comments she made about it, but the words still rang in my mind as I drove north the following morning.

I dawdled on the way to the cabin. I had forgotten to take a toothbrush, and stopped in a shopping center to buy one. I stopped again for fruit juice and eggs, cheese and whole wheat bread for later in the week when I planned to break my fast. I was afraid to go to the cabin alone.

It was nearly nightfall when I finally arrived. I lit the pilot light on the hot water heater and turned on the refrigerator. The cabin was cold, damp, and musty. A large stone fireplace dominated the sitting room, but it didn't work. I couldn't figure out how to light the oil heater. The people to whom I was instructed to go for help were away from the lake for the weekend and would not return for another twenty-four hours.

I brought my supplies and belongings into the cabin: a few groceries, a bag of warm clothing, my sleeping bag, and my books. Besides Elizabeth O'Connor's books, I had *Hey God, What Do I Do Now?* by Jess Lair,[3] a commentary on the Gospel of John, a textbook for beginning Greek, my Bible, and a stack of notebooks containing over a thousand pages of my own journal writing. I thought if I read my old journals, I might be able to figure out how I had gone astray and find the inspiration I had somehow lost. Unpacking and settling down in the cabin took less than an hour. Time crawled and stretched endlessly before me. Since I was fasting, I could not pass the time with cooking and eating. I made some tea, did some calisthenics to warm myself, and climbed into my sleeping bag with *Hey God.*

I did not really understand the central message of the book. Instead, certain sentences that reinforced my preoccupations assailed me. The first sentence that stood out was, "I am unable to love; therefore you are alone." It seemed to be true in my situation. My husband was alone and my daughters were alone. The Next Door was alone, and the guests who came there were alone. As I wrote in my journal that night, I asked myself how I came to be unable to love. I was plagued by lack of acceptance for myself and weighed down with guilt and resentment. I knew I was going to wrestle with my own demons in that cabin, and held on for dear life to the affirmation, "Jesus is Lord, and we are His."

That night I had a dream. In the dream I was at home and at The Next Door. Everywhere I turned I was haunted by the only young woman I had ever really hated. She was begging for food because she was too lazy and disorganized to get food stamps. Everyone else in the dream was helping her and treating her well. I refused to help, and the others were angry with me. Still she hounded me. I awoke crying because I could not get away from her.

After drinking the decaffeinated coffee which constituted my

breakfast, I conducted a counseling session with myself in my
journal. A dream figure that appeared so vividly was certainly
a reflection of myself. I identified the similarities between the
dream image and me. I seemed always to be begging for something—as she did. I failed to appreciate what was given to
me—so did she. I managed my household very little better than
she had. The main reason my life was different from hers was
that my mate had a steady job and a good income. He had
money, and went out to purchase groceries himself. My house
was easier to keep in a livable condition, and my husband did
most of the work. It was not she but myself whom I really hated.
Until I learned to accept what she represented, I would be
haunted by self-hatred wherever I went.

Elizabeth O'Connor wrote that self-hatred was incompatible
with Christianity. If one hated oneself, one was either holding
apart awareness of sin or denying the love of God. I even hated
myself for hating myself. Unable to resolve the tangle of thoughts
and feelings, I went for a long walk.

By late afternoon, the neighbors who could help me light the
heater had still not returned home. I was not doing at all well
with austerity. Being cold and hungry on top of hating myself
was not doing me any good. I gave in to my weakness, climbed
into my nice warm car, drove to town, bought myself a nice
warm hamburger, and went to a nice warm movie! By the time
I returned, there was a light in the neighboring cottage. I asked
for help, and finally had heat.

During the days that followed, I ate light meals and read. I
also did calisthenics and lengthened my walks to encompass the
entire lake, a distance of about six miles.

As I read my old journals I was reminded of a visual phenomenon I had experienced from time to time in years past, a kind
of hallucination I suppose. During stressful times I would glance
at an object and it would seem to twinkle and shower me with
particles of light. Most frequently the object was a birch tree
growing beside a lake. The leaves on birches are often shiny
dark green on one side and nearly white on the other. Sunlight

on the water sparkles, and the combination of heat and stress could easily cause my brain to superimpose one image on another.

I had a friend who was diagnosed as schizophrenic and suffered from hallucinations. She once described to me the same visual phenomenon. For reasons she could not explain, she was terrified by the experience. For her the particules of light were like a snowstorm which threatened to engulf her. She would have given anything to have stopped seeing it. The same vision filled me with inexplicable delight. It seemed to me the most exquisite sight that eyes could ever see. For me it represented the glory of God shining through the cosmos. I would have given anything to have been able to see it again!

I read in a book whose title and author I cannot remember that the difference between a mystic and a schizophrenic is the capacity of the former for sheer drudgery. My friend was immobilized by her hallucination; I was empowered by mine. Indeed, without it, the most interesting job imaginable had become unbearable drudgery. This experience had not occurred for over a year. Since I never talked about it, I had forgotten it. More than anything in the world, I wanted to see a birch tree twinkle! If only I could see once more that incredible beauty, I felt that I could face the demands of daily life and be happy.

As I pondered the question of what prevented me from seeing birch trees twinkle, two possibilities emerged. My discipline of prayer had fallen by the wayside along with my disciplines of diet and exercise. I was unpracticed in generating a state of mind in which I was receptive to such a phenomenon. The quiet inner space at my core was no longer open to divine light, but was instead crowded by my own psychological needs and those of others. Even in the relatively soundless atmosphere of the cabin, my mind was not quiet. I kept thinking about people at home and at The Next Door. These memories and images did not come to me of their own accord. I invited them to fill the silence. My interactions with them had become a kind of idolatry, and I used them to bolster my faltering ego. In order to pray with my whole heart, I had to remove these shadows of other people from my mind.

Reminding myself constantly that "Jesus is Lord and we are His," I summoned all my counseling skills to clean house psychologically, to rid myself of these fragmented projections of myself which I had come to need and idolize. One by one, I called the symbolic figures to mind, imagined them in the room with me, held conversations with them, and bid them farewell. From a psychological standpoint, this was a dangerous thing for me to do alone and in the state of mind I was in. I had been dependent upon those people, my husband and friends and enemies alike, for my sense of self-worth. Separate from them I had no reason to go on living. In the space between cutting myself off from human relationships and centering myself in prayer, I was extremely vulnerable.

Late Wednesday afternoon, Barbie and her mother stopped by to see how I was doing. Perhaps sensing how depressed I was, they invited me to spend the evening with them in town. By that time, I was thoroughly committed to emptying my mind of all human conversation. Talk had become odious to me. I could barely keep track of what they were saying and reply coherently.

I was unable to turn off my mental tape recording of their brief visit after they left. Barbie was precisely the kind of person I wished I could be. She was kind and accepting; she was energetic and hard working. She was not bookish and introspective like me; she was not egotistical and dependent upon the opinions of others like me. If I were like Barbie, I could work all day at The Next Door and come home and clean house and bake bread at night. Everyone would be happy: my husband, my kids, and the people at the Next Door. Marlin deserved a wife like Barbie; The Next Door deserved a director like Barbie. Barbie would be happy with all of the advantages of my life which I held in such disdain. I did not deserve all those advantages. I did not deserve even to live. The world, I thought, would be a better place without the likes of me. I looked at the rat poison. Overwhelmed as I was with guilt, ingesting it seemed the decent thing to do.

The sun was setting. Darkness and silence closed in around me as I began to contemplate my own death. I felt that I was forever incapable of enjoying life, incapable of functioning and accomplishing anything. I read the labels on the boxes of rat poison. The discomfort that would result from taking it seemed insignificant compared with the self-torture of being isolated, purposeless, and without a single virtue to justify my existence.

Still, I did not want to die. I wanted to believe that Jesus is Lord and that I belonged to Him. I wanted to fulfill the chief end of humankind as described in the Westminster Catechism: to glorify God and to enjoy God forever. I wanted to see a birch tree twinkle. I paced the floor and wept. "Seek and ye shall find," I screamed at my tortured soul. "Knock and the door will be opened! Ask and it will be given you!" Sobbing violently, I knelt beside the old sofa in front of the defunct fireplace. "Where are You?" I prayed aloud. "I've been seeking and I can't find You. I've been knocking and the door won't open. I've been asking and nothing has been given to me. I can't go on living without You. I want You to be here with me now, and give me a reason not to take the rat poison!" I pounded the sofa cushion and continued to sob.

Then I felt a whisper in the back of my head. I paused momentarily, and resumed my sobbing. Then I said aloud, "Wait a minute. I think I heard something. If You're with me, speak again." Behind my closed eyelids I saw a glimmer of light. From the deep recesses of my mind I heard an unintelligible sound which I somehow understood.

Aloud I said, "Let me see if I heard You right. You have something You want me to do for You." I felt that I had understood correctly.

In the same way that I had imagined all the other people to be in the cottage speaking with me, I imagined the light and the voice outside myself and present in the room so that I could speak to it. The image I mentally projected was faceless, a warm white light that floated slightly above me. "You have something You want me to do for You," I said over and over, astonished. "Why me? I'm so messed up!"

The light laughed.

"Okay," I said. "You have something You want me to do for You, and why You want me is Your own private joke. I can go along with that. That's as good a reason as I can think of to do something. What is it You want me to do?"

The light made a gesture that reminded me of a shrug of the shoulders, but I felt at the same time that the gesture meant that everything was as it should be.

"All right. What You want from me is not a specific thing, not a particular heroic or dramatic act. You want me to keep on doing what I am doing and fit into the scheme of things. Eventually I'll catch on to the humor or the purpose in it. Right?"

I had received what I had asked for. It wasn't quite what I expected. I had expected some marvelous sensation of twinkling birches, the comforting assurance that I was loved. Instead, I was playing guessing games with a figment of my imagination which was beginning to seem quite real. I was afraid that I was insane. I was even more afraid that I was not insane and was indeed having an encounter with the Paraclete of the Fourth Gospel. What does one say to an omnipotent God? Perhaps I should try to remember a ritual prayer, the kind of thing people had addressed to God through the centuries.

The light laughed again.

I understood immediately the humor in my thoughts. It didn't matter what I said aloud because He heard my thoughts. At worst, I would see myself for the silly, trivial creature that I was. I had spent much of my life trying to explain myself to other people who never fully understood. I suddenly felt myself to be completely understood and with no need to explain anything. More than anything at that moment, I wanted that Being to stay with me.

"I can hardly believe you're spending so much time with me!" I blurted out apologetically.

Once more the light laughed.

I laughed too. "What am I saying? I'm used to people who are important being too busy for me. You literally have all the time in the world. You're eternal. To You nothing is a waste of time."

I had the distinct feeling that the Spirit I visualized as light was pleased to stay.

Suddenly, I was incredibly hungry. "As long as You are in no hurry to leave, You won't mind, will You, if I get something to eat?" Our Lord was always willing to sit at table with publicans and sinners. Perhaps they, too, made Him laugh. When I had prepared soup and bread and cheese, I said, "I know a Hebrew blessing. I went to a lot of trouble to memorize it so that I could hear how the syllables sounded when You broke bread. 'Baruch atta Adonoi. . . .' "

The light shrugged, but everything was not as it should have been.

"Oh, I'm sorry. I was showing off. I should have realized. You don't care about the language because You're beyond language. You care about what we mean in our hearts. I pray better in English. 'Blessed art Thou, O Lord, Our God, Sovereign of the universe, who has kept us in life and sustained us and hast brought us to this season.' " I had been kept in life and sustained and brought into table fellowship with the Lord, and I felt profoundly grateful.

I felt a need to keep talking, but was having trouble thinking of things to say. "As long as You're here, do you mind if I ask You a few questions?"

He didn't seem to mind.

"This kind of private audience with You isn't very Presbyterian," I continued. "What about Community?"

I had the feeling I should keep talking and put an answer into my own words. "I guess I wouldn't know whom I was talking to without the Community of faith that taught me. I probably would not have called on You for help without it. I am part of a community even here. I wouldn't be here if it weren't for

Barbie and her parents, if not for Sharon and Nico, who are probably praying for me right now. Nor would I have a job or a calling or know what You want me to keep on doing without the Community. Communal prayer is empty without this sense of being close to You in a personal way. But this personal imminence would go awry or dissipate without its being vali-dated by the community and expressed in and through it."

I felt satisfied with my answer.

"Okay, now that we've established that it's really okay for me to be sitting here talking to You like this, how do I know You're really here?"

The light laughed again.

"Of course, that's silly. You are because You are. The great 'I Am.' But how do I know that what You are saying to me really comes from You?"

The light shrugged.

"You aren't saying anything to me. You are beyond words. You speak in creation and redemption. All the words took form in my own mind. Anything that comes through our minds is finite and timebound· What seems to be true to me right now may or may not be true for anyone else at any other time. I can't go around claiming that You told me anything. All I can know is that there is something that is redemptive behind the images my mind projects and behind the words I hear in my mind. At least what is happening is redemptive in the sense that it gets me through the night. At any rate, I'm not going to take rat poison!"

Once more I felt satisfied with my answer. I thanked Him. My mind was beginning to wander. Faces and voices of the people in my life began to crowd into my consciousness.

"What am I supposed to do with all those people?" I asked. "Most of all, what am I going to do about Marlin? I don't see how I can keep going, continuing to work on The Next Door without his giving me a little emotional support."

The light gestured once more for me to answer my own question.

"Marlin loves me. Even if he doesn't understand, he isn't going to leave me. I think You are trying to tell me that You'll take care of Marlin."

I mentioned several other people with whom I had difficulties and felt the same answer. I continued to chatter, to ask questions, to experiment. Part of the time I simply enjoyed the silence. For the first time in years I was at peace with myself. As I relaxed, I felt extremely tired.

Finally I said, "Say, could You do me a favor? Just a little one? You know how excited I get when I see the birch trees twinkle. Could you, please, let me see that again just once before I go home?"

The light laughed again.

"I think this kind of personal encounter is too much for my mind to sustain for very long. You appeared to Moses in a burning bush, and I guess I'm asking You to go hide Yourself back in the bushes!"

I was exhausted by my days and nights of self-torture, and needed very badly to sleep. I went to bed, and closed my eyes. All I could think to say was the familiar child's prayer, "Now I lay me down to sleep. . . ."

During the following days, the Presence was still with me in a general way. I prayed and felt that I was heard. I continued my regimen of diet and exercise. Reading and studying came easily. Ideas flowed together and made sense to me. I thought about the people in my life, and forgave them and felt that I was forgiven. I felt loving and peaceful toward them because I was no longer dependent upon them for my sense of self worth and usefulness. I thought about my family and knew that somehow Marlin and I would be reconciled. I thought about The Next Door and felt able to face the people there again. I felt more peace and health than I had ever felt before.

On Saturday morning the time had come for me to leave the cottage by the lake. I felt sad because I had come to love the place. I also felt sad that I had not seen a birch tree twinkle, although I had looked for this to happen whenever I was out of doors. I cleaned the cabin, turned off the utility tanks and the refrigerator, packed my belongings into the car, and locked the cabin door.

There was really no need for me to hurry home. After I returned the key to Barbie's parents' home, I ate a leisurely lunch in a restaurant. As I drove down the highway along the Lake Michigan shoreline, I thought about the birch trees. I stopped at a state park, left the car, and walked along the beach. The sun shone; the sand and water sparkled. The scene was beautiful and bright with natural light. The dunes were dotted with birch trees, and the leaves fluttered in the breeze. I sat down and gazed from one end of the beach to the other, awaiting a miracle. I thought and prayed and daydreamed there on the beach, squinting at the shining water until my eyes hurt, and then looked at the trees. I stared at the sand. Bits of silicone glistened, but nothing else happened. I waited for hours, trying every mental trick I could think of to see what I wanted to see. The sun moved toward the horizon beyond the great lake, and I knew that I should soon leave the beach and drive the rest of the distance home.

Becoming impatient, I decided to take a hike along the shore. I passed a few people who are beginning to shiver in their attempt to get a tan so early in the season. After half a mile, I noticed a path up the dune to my right. I had almost given up on the birch trees, but I scrambled up the steep dune just the same. When I reached the top and looked across the gulf to the next dune, I saw a large grove of birch trees ablaze with twinkling light. It looked like an explosion in a fireworks factory; I had never seen so many birch trees twinkle so intensely in my whole life! I fell on my knees and wept for joy. I looked away because It was too beautiful for my eyes to stand. When I looked back, they kept right on twinkling and showering me with radiant white light. I drank in the vision for at least fifteen minutes, filling my soul with it, until the sand and the lake twinkled too. Everything on which I rested my eyes twinkled all the way home.

As I drove I contemplated the change in myself. A mere seven days earlier I was thoroughly burned out. In one short week I had learned several important things. My desperation was not so much a product of the difficulty of the work and the stressful environment as it was a product of my own weaknesses. Neither success in working nor the encouragement of other people could be depended upon to strengthen me. The strength I required to sustain me was available from one source alone: "Jesus is Lord and we are His."

NOTES

1. O'Connor, Elizabeth. *Search For Silence.* Waco, Texas: Word Books, 1973.

2. O'Connor, Elizabeth. *Eighth Day of Creation: Gifts and Creativity.* Waco, Texas: Word Books, 1971.

3. Lair, Jess. *Hey God, What Should I Do Now?* Greenwich, Connecticut: Fawcett Publishing Company, 1973.

DATE DUE